D1218100

GRADIENT
Style

COLOR-SHIFTING
TECHNIQUES
& KNITTING PATTERNS

 Interweave

a content + ecommerce company

WWW.FWCOMMUNITY.COM

WWW.INTERWEAVE.COM

22 21 20 19 18   5 4 3 2 1

SRN: 18KN05
ISBN-13: 978-1-63250-650-4

EDITORIAL DIRECTOR Kerry Bogert

EDITOR Maya Elson

TECHNICAL EDITOR Therese Chynoweth

ART DIRECTOR Ashlee Wadeson

INTERIOR DESIGNER Pamela Norman

ILLUSTRATOR Therese Chynoweth

PHOTOGRAPHER
Harper Point; George Boe

STYLIST Allie Liebgott

HAIR AND MAKEUP Liz Wegrzyn

CONTENTS

INTRODUCTION

WHETHER YOU CALL it ombré, fade, or gradient, the beauty of creating color-shifting projects has been a revelation for modern knitters. Thanks to gifted designers and amazing dyers with an eye for color, we're able to apply a whole new spectrum of possibilities to our knitting projects.

As much fun as colorful knits can be, knitting with three, five, or even ten colors can be intimidating. The thought of choosing perfectly combined colors might cause you to freeze, or past unsuccessful attempts at color blending might have you shying away from the bold choices inherent in gradient designs. The truth is, if you've ever thought: "That pattern is so pretty, but I don't know what colors I'd choose," you are not alone.

Fear no more, the editors at Interweave have got your color questions covered. *Gradient Style* is your guide to understanding the fundamentals of the color wheel, what to do with those long gradient skeins, and how to choose and blend colors for visually seamless color changes. With a few simple techniques, you'll be adding stunning color combinations to your projects. Whether it's a simple stockinette-stitch tee worked from a cool gradient pack or a one-of-a-kind brioche stitch cowl knit with hand-dyed speckled skeins, the projects in this book are your chance to experiment and have fun playing with color.

If you're already a knitting-with-color guru, there is no doubt the nineteen inspiring projects will keep your needles entertained with an array of garments and accessories. You can knit the patterns as written or use one of the gradient methods shared in Getting Started with Gradients to stitch something extra special.

Grab your needles and yarn and give in to a gradient project. You're sure to have a riot—both of color and fun!

Kerry Bogert

Knitter and Editorial Director
Interweave Books

GETTING STARTED
WITH GRADIENTS

o·················o

by **Emma Welford**

THE DESIGNERS WHO created the gorgeous garments and accessories showcased in this collection have taken a wide variety of gradient, variegated, solid, and semisolid yarns and combined them in myriad ways to create innovative knitted designs. They have done the work for you in figuring out how to feature gradient color schemes in the most effective (and fun to knit!) ways. But not everyone has the same taste in yarn and colors. You might love

a project knit in colors on the warm end of the spectrum, but you prefer to wear cool colors.

How can you substitute yarns or colors in a pattern or create your own gradient designs? This section takes the mystery out of creating gradient color schemes. It first delves into the color wheel and ways to use it to create harmonious color schemes, including taking advantage of values, tints, and undertones.

You'll then learn a variety of techniques for knitting gradient patterns, including even striping, uneven striping, and double stranding. Finally, the exciting possibilities and challenges of combining gradient color schemes with stranded colorwork are explored. Let's get started!

Making Your Own Gradient Palette

COMMERCIALLY DYED yarns that knit up into colorful gradients are undeniably attractive and a wonderful option for creating a fade effect. But it can be even more satisfying to create your own by blending colors and yarns of your choosing.

If you've never played with color, the idea of creating your own gradient may feel daunting. But gradients are, in fact, a great starting point for experimenting with color—especially colors you are attracted to but don't necessarily wear very often. You can choose one such color as a focal point of your gradient or use it as an accent, working it into your palette with speckles and flashes of color.

HELPFUL TOOLS & APPROACHES

A color wheel is a great tool to have on hand as you get comfortable experimenting with color. It shows you how colors fall along the spectrum and their technical categories to help identify how colors will work together. There are also many websites and apps that will automatically create color palettes based on various selections you make.

Nothing compares to physically playing with yarn to develop your gradient, and I suggest making a trip to your local yarn store whenever possible to do just that. When using hand-dyed yarns in particular, it's helpful to observe the nuances from skein to skein in person, rather than through a computer screen. Unless the dyer's website showcases a full knitted swatch of the skein, you might be surprised at some of the colors that pop up when working with hand-dyed yarns.

CHOOSING COLORS

Your ultimate goal when choosing a color palette for a gradient is different from choosing a palette for a standard striped or stranded colorwork project. While most types of colorwork knitting rely on contrast to make the motifs pop, a gradient or faded look requires seamless color blending. There are several techniques for manipulating the transition between colors (see Gradient Techniques), but you'll have better success choosing a color palette with a general gradient in mind, rather than trying to shoehorn random colors into a gradient.

First, let's cover some basic color theory. Refer to the color wheel as you read through these definitions. We'll refer to these terms throughout this chapter.

- Primary colors are red, yellow, and blue. All other colors are created by combining two or more of these colors.

- Secondary colors (orange, green, and purple) are created by combining two primary colors.

- Tertiary colors are created by mixing a primary and secondary color, such as combining yellow and green to create a yellow-green.

- Tints are created by adding white to a base color.

- Shades are created by adding black to a base color.

- Tones are created by adding gray to a base color.

- Complementary colors are colors opposite each other on the color wheel, such as green and red.

- Analogous colors are colors next to each other on the color wheel, such as green and yellow.

- Triadic colors are colors spaced equally apart on the color wheel, such as green, orange, and purple.

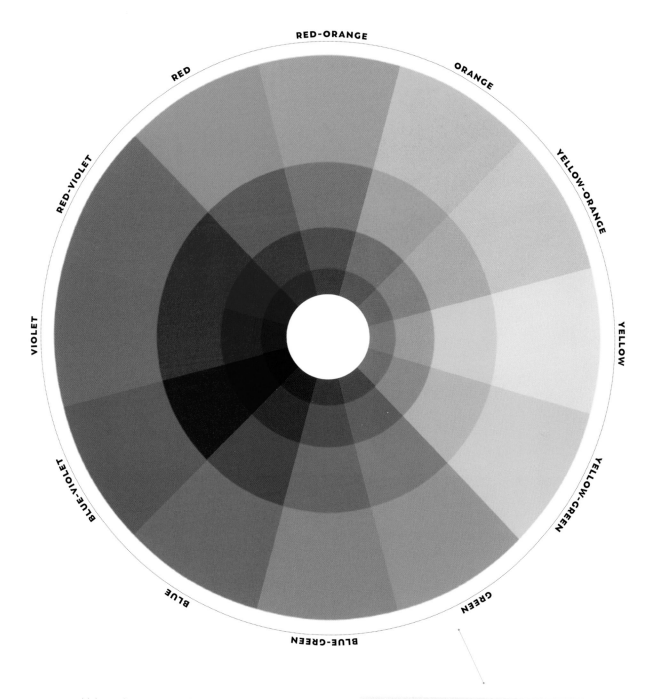

RED-ORANGE

RED

ORANGE

RED-VIOLET

YELLOW-ORANGE

VIOLET

YELLOW

BLUE-VIOLET

YELLOW-GREEN

BLUE

GREEN

BLUE-GREEN

- Value refers to a color's lightness or darkness.

To begin, pick one or two colors to "ground" your gradient—i.e., the color or colors you want at either end of your gradient. If you want to base your gradient around a single color, you only need to pick the color you want at one end of your gradient.

THIS COLOR WHEEL shows the twelve main colors of the spectrum. The shades are shown in the inner two rings, the pure hues are placed in the next ring, and the tints are in the outer ring.

ANALOGOUS COLOR GRADIENTS

If you want to base your gradient around two or more colors, you will focus on creating a smooth hue shift rather than a light-to-dark fade of just one color. An easy place to start for this hue-shift style is by choosing two analogous colors, such as red and orange (shown on the opposite page), and blending them with as many intermediary shades as you like to complete the gradient.

Analogous colors create an appealing gradient, and in my opinion look very natural compared to more complicated gradients. The more colors you add between your end colors, the more gradual the gradient will appear. You can use speckles, flashes, and other brief spots of color to aid and soften the color shifts.

TIP *Try combining the light-to-dark nature of a monochromatic palette with the hue shift of an analogous palette by choosing colors with different values in your color shift. A yellow-to-green analogous palette can have more depth if the gradient starts with a pale pastel yellow and ends in a deep forest green.*

MONOCHROMATIC GRADIENTS

By using tints and shades, you can create a monochromatic gradient (above), which blends from light to dark within one color. This style of gradient is the easiest option to make and wear, since all the colors will have the same undertones and look harmonious together.

A gradient running from light gray to black is a classic monochromatic gradient. You can add both tints and shades to your base color to create a dramatic monochromatic palette that spans from very light to very dark, or you can focus on either tints or shades to create a narrower color range. For example, a monochromatic palette based on a sky blue color with only white tints added would create a very light and airy pastel palette.

undertones

The first thing you'll notice in any color is its main tone—"that's blue." An undertone is the influence of other colors underneath that color. These are referred to as cool (blue, green, or purple), warm (red, yellow, or orange), or neutral (a mix of cool and warm tones). These undertones are an important consideration for monochromatic and analogous gradients. You can achieve different visual effects by keeping the undertones consistent throughout the gradient or purposely mixing them up to add another layer of contrast. For example:

A monochromatic gradient of cool pale blue to cool dark blue has consistent undertones.

A monochromatic gradient of cool pale blue to warm dark blue has mixed undertones.

An analogous gradient of warm red to warm orange has consistent undertones.

An analogous gradient of cool red to warm orange has mixed undertones.

COMPLEMENTARY COLOR GRADIENTS

Complementary colors (those on opposite sides of the color wheel) are a great starting point for dynamic color-shifting gradients. The best way to blend complementary colors is to choose analogous colors that fall between them on the color wheel to smooth the transition between these two very different shades; speckled or variegated colors are very useful here.

For example, when fading from purple to yellow, look for speckles or flashes of yellow and other warm colors in the colors closer to the purple end of the spectrum. This helps tie the full gradient together by adding a small yet consistent thread throughout your palette. Think of it as a sub-gradient within your larger overall palette.

RANDOM COLORS

If you've fallen in love with two colors that are not analogous or complementary, don't worry! You can use the technique of looking for speckles or flashes of similar colors to bridge the transition. For example, take a look at the palette used for the swatches in Gradient Techniques.

This palette goes from light gray to teal in an unexpected and fun way by mixing in speckles of brown, orange, and pink to create a unique gradient that looks cohesive.

With practice and swatching, you'll be better able to tell which gradients will and won't work when you shop for yarn.

COUSTEAU *is a solid teal and the darkest color in this gradient combination.*

UNDERGROWTH *is a semisolid teal that mixes well with the blue speckles in Video Baby.*

VIDEO BABY *is a speckled mix of orange, blue, brown, and pink.*

CONFERENCE CALL *features a light gray base that coordinates with Great Grey Owl and blue and brown speckles that echo Video Baby.*

GREAT GREY OWL *is a semisolid light gray.*

(All of the yarns shown here and in the swatches that follow are Madelinetosh Tosh Merino Light Yarn.)

Gradient Techniques

Once you've chosen your color palette, you are ready to begin knitting your gradient. There are several methods for blending colors, depending on the project and the look you're trying to achieve.

If you're following a pattern that incorporates a gradient, the designer will usually provide detailed instructions for how to get the look displayed in their project. However, if you're modifying a one-color garment into a gradient, or if you'd like to try a different gradient than suggested, you can experiment with the methods outlined here. Note that if you're modifying an existing pattern, you'll need to calculate how many rows will

be in the total piece based on your row gauge and use that to determine when to switch colors in your gradient for a balanced look. (Or, use that information to create a purposely unbalanced look, such as a gradient yoke on a solid-body sweater.)

Many factors contribute to how seamless your gradient will look— your colors chosen, your personal gauge, and the pattern itself. Swatch several gradient methods to see which works best with your color palette; you may find that one method hides color changes well while another makes the color shifts more obvious. Of course, if you prefer the random look of occasional striping or pooling, you can purposely choose a method that delivers these results.

EVEN STRIPING (WORKED FLAT)

Work even in color A (Great Grey Owl shown here) until ready to change colors.

*Work 2 rows with color B (Conference Call shown here).

Work 2 rows with color A.

Repeat from * once more.

Work even in color B until ready to change colors.

Repeat color change sequence with color C (Video Baby, shown here), and so on throughout your gradient.

You'll see that the gradient is practically invisible between the first three colors. Once D (Cousteau) is introduced into the mix, its first two rows blend with Video Baby but its successive rows are more visible. This is simply due to the unexpected nature of hand-dyed yarn, as the first two rows of Cousteau happen to coincide with a particularly blue-heavy section of Video Baby, which camouflages the stripe. It's still an excellent way to combine semisolid and speckled colors if you are comfortable with the possibility of occasional visible transitions.

Somehow this doesn't work as well with only semisolid colors (see swatch at right). While these three colors are attractive together and could be included in the same gradient with additional transition colors, they create obvious stripes on their own. Great Grey Owl and Undergrowth are simply too far apart from each other, and Undergrowth and Cousteau, though more similar, lack enough common tones to create a blended effect.

FROM LIGHTEST TO DARKEST:
Great Grey Owl (A), Conference Call (B), Video Baby (C), Cousteau (D)

FROM LIGHTEST TO DARKEST:
Great Grey Owl (A), Undergrowth (B), Cousteau (C)

UNEVEN STRIPING (WORKED FLAT)

Work even in color A (Great Grey Owl shown here) until ready to change colors.

Work 2 rows with color B (Conference Call shown here).

Work 4 rows with color A.

Work 4 rows with color B.

Work 2 rows with color A.

Work even in color B until ready to change colors.

Repeat the color change sequence with color C (Video Baby shown here), and so on throughout your gradient.

This method works best with highly variegated or speckled palettes. Notice that Conference Call and Video Baby transition well, even with the four-row stretches of transition, but the two semi solid colors (Great Grey Owl and Cousteau) don't fare as well. With a fully speckled palette, this method is ideal for creating extra-long blends of color for a more gradual gradient.

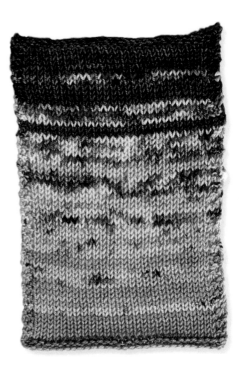

FROM LIGHTEST TO DARKEST:
Great Grey Owl (A), Conference Call (B), Video Baby (C), Cousteau (D)

FROM LIGHTEST TO DARKEST:
Undergrowth (A), Cousteau (B)

DOUBLE STRANDING (WORKED FLAT)

Work even with 2 strands of color A (Undergrowth shown here) until ready to change colors.

Work even with 1 strand of color A and 1 strand of color B (Cousteau shown here) until ready to change colors.

Work even with 2 strands of color B until ready to change colors.

Shown here with only two colors, you can still use this technique to cover a whole palette's worth of fading. Double stranding is ideal for lighter-weight yarns, especially when substituting a lighter-weight yarn than is called for in a pattern. It works well to blend semi-solids, as shown here, and is most successful with monochromatic or analogous palettes.

TINY STRIPES
(WORKED IN THE ROUND)

Work even in color A (Great Grey Owl shown here) until ready to change colors.

*Work 1 row with color B (Conference Call shown here).

Work 1 row with color A.

Repeat from * twice more.

Work even in color B until ready to change colors.

Repeat color change sequence with color C (Video Baby shown here), and so on throughout your gradient.

Working in the round allows for narrow one-round stripes, which can help blend stubborn colors and cover a shorter distance with your gradient, since it takes a small number of rounds overall. However, as in the examples for Methods 1 and 2, Cousteau still stands out and creates visible stripes.

FROM LIGHTEST TO DARKEST: *Great Grey Owl (A), Conference Call (B), Video Baby, Cousteau (C)*

Colorwork & Color Placement

STRANDED COLORWORK projects are a great place to showcase a gradient. You can pair a gradient with a solid color or work with two gradients simultaneously to play with as much color as possible. However, you'll need to keep value in mind for stranded colorwork projects. In other words, if you viewed your colors in gray scale, would they look closer to white or closer to black?

Thanks to the digital age, it's quick and easy to figure out your color's value. Simply take a photo of a color combination you are considering and convert the image to gray-scale to view the value of the colors. Is there noticeable contrast between your colors, or do they all appear a similar shade of gray?

Contrasting values (light next to dark) will show off your stranded motif most clearly, while values that are too similar to each other will obscure the motif. If you want the motif to be visible above all else, you can choose a gradient with light-to-medium values and a solid contrasting color with a dark value. If you want to play with the appearance of the colorwork motif fading in and out of the gradient, you could choose a contrasting color with a value that matches the value of one of your gradient colors. I like to pick a contrasting color that coordinates with one of the colors in the gradient, whether an exact match for a muddled gradient or a noticeably darker/lighter version for a clear gradient. You can also add more visual interest by choosing a solid color that is complementary to one or more colors in your gradient.

Single-skein gradients are very convenient and can really shine in stranded colorwork projects. They not only eliminate the need to calculate when to change colors, but also don't produce multiple ends to weave in at each color change. You can simply focus on your stranded or intarsia pattern, which makes your knitting experience less stressful.

Of course, if you want to use two gradients at the same time (as in the Spectrum Hat shown at right), you're adding a whole new level of complication to this process! As in the previous example, decide if you want the motifs to be clear or occasionally obstructed and use that information to guide your palette choices.

- For clear motifs, choose palettes with no color overlap and no value overlap. Gradient 1 could blend from white to gold, while gradient 2 could blend from cobalt blue to black.

- For muddled motifs, choose palettes with at least one color overlap and/or one value overlap. You could even use the same palette, just starting at different ends of the gradient! This will ensure a harmonious look, as all the colors work well together, and will create an opportunity for one or more sections where the motif fades into the background.

While using two gradients at once requires some thoughtful planning, the end result pays off immensely by creating an undulating and mesmerizing effect. Especially if you use two single-skein gradient yarns, you'll have a showpiece that really didn't take much extra effort on your part— but you can still take all the credit.

the PROJECTS

ONE OF THE wonderful things about knitting with gradients is that there is no limit to the patterns and stitch techniques you can use. Combining a gradient pattern can take a common knitting pattern or technique and elevate it to new levels of sophistication and fun! The original designs in this collection highlight many of these possibilities.

You'll find patterns for a wide variety of scarves, shawls, cardigans, hats, cowls worked in lace, cables, intarsia, slip-stitch, stranded knitting, and more. Double stranding with several colors creates a gradient pattern that softens bold color-blocked mittens. Stranded knitting achieves a beautiful subtlety when worked with gradients in a pair of gorgeous rose-patterned socks. A bold gradient that travels from deep blue to bright yellow transforms a simple stockinette pullover into a showstopper. These are just a few of the many exciting patterns created by our team of talented designers.

OMBRÉ EYELET *stole*

Working a combination of simple slipped stitches and
yarnover results in a textured fabric with interest on both
sides. Two gradient yarns are worked in opposite directions—
one from dark to light, the second from light to dark—creating
a striking ombré effect with the darkest shades at the two
bottom edges. The simple rectangular shape showcases the
hypnotic color pattern. • **Susanna IC**

FINISHED SIZE

16" (40.5 cm) wide and 54" (137 cm) long.

YARN

Fingering weight (#1 Super Fine).

Shown here: KnitCircus Trampoline (100% superwash merino wool; 440 yd [402 m]/3½ oz [100 g]):

Pumpkin Spice Latte (MC), 1 skein; Orange You Glad (CC), 1 skein.

NEEDLES

Size U.S. 7 (4.5 mm).

Adjust needle size if necessary to achieve the correct gauge.

NOTIONS

Tapestry needle.

GAUGE

20 sts and 35 rows = 4" (10 cm) in patt, blocked.

NOTES

• The stole is worked in one piece from end to end.

• All four sides are worked with yarn over edgings for easy blocking—the blocking wires can be threaded through the yarnovers.

• Stitches are always slipped with yarn at the wrong side of work.

• Colors change every two rows; loosely carry the unused yarn along the right edge.

Stole

With MC, loosely CO 79 sts.

Next row: (WS) Knit.

Row 1: (RS) *K2tog, yo; rep from * to last st, k1.

Rows 2, 4, 6, and 8: (WS) Knit.

Rows 3, 5, and 7: K2tog, yo, knit to last 2 sts, yo, ssk.

Join CC.

Set-up row: (RS) Working Row 1 of chart, beg at right edge of Eyelet Chart, work first 3 sts, rep next 4 sts to last 4 sts, then work 4 sts at left edge of chart.

Next row: (WS) Working Row 2 of chart, beg at left edge of chart, work first 4 sts, rep next 4 sts to last 3 sts, then work 3 sts at right edge of chart.

Cont as established, work Rows 3–8, then rep Rows 1–8 fifty-four more times, changing colors as directed.

EYELET CHART

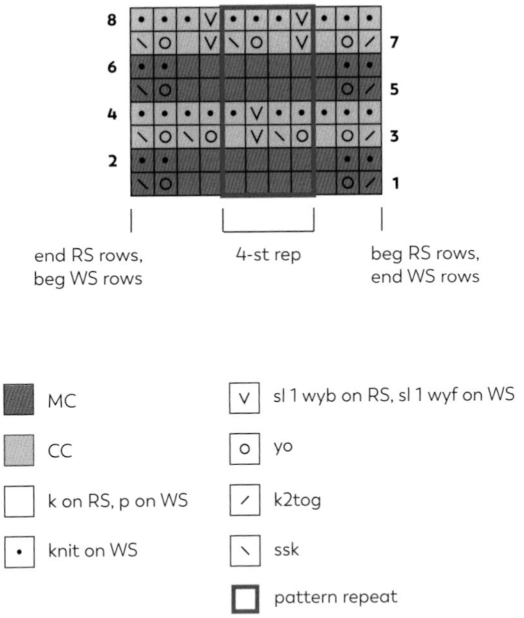

end RS rows, beg WS rows

4-st rep

beg RS rows, end WS rows

	MC			V	sl 1 wyb on RS, sl 1 wyf on WS
	CC			o	yo
	k on RS, p on WS			/	k2tog
•	knit on WS			\	ssk
					pattern repeat

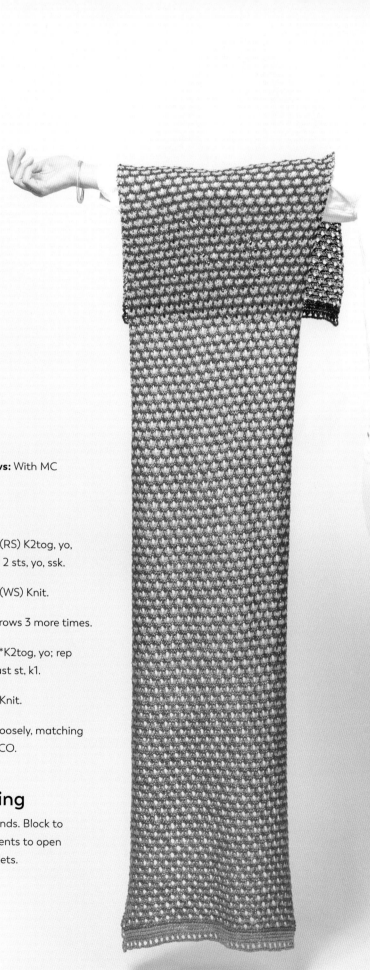

Next 2 rows: With MC only, knit.

Cut MC.

Next row: (RS) K2tog, yo, knit to last 2 sts, yo, ssk.

Next row: (WS) Knit.

Rep last 2 rows 3 more times.

Next row: *K2tog, yo; rep from * to last st, k1.

Next row: Knit.

BO all sts loosely, matching tension of CO.

Finishing

Weave in ends. Block to measurements to open up the eyelets.

SPRING COLORS *tee*

This quick-and-easy spring top is worked from the bottom up and is almost entirely seamless. It's perfect for the warming days before summer is in full swing or early fall when it's not quite cool enough for a sweater. An analogous color pattern that transitions from a brilliant blue to a vibrant yellow elevates the simple design into a striking work of art. • **Alyssa Cabrera**

FINISHED SIZES

43 (45¾, 51¾, 55¼, 59)" (109 [116, 131.5, 140.5, 150] cm) bust circumference and 19¼ (21, 21¼, 24¼, 24¾)" (49 [53.5, 54, 61.5, 63] cm) long.

Tee shown measures 43" (109 cm).

YARN

Fingering Weight (#1 Super Fine).

Shown here: Done Roving Frolicking Feet Mini Gradients (100% superwash merino wool; 600 yd [549 m]/5¼ oz [150 g]): Maine Marsh (colors in kit labeled A through F, with A being the darkest and F being the lightest), 2 (3, 3, 4, 4) kits.

NEEDLES

Size U.S. 4 (3.5 mm): 32" (80 cm) circular (cir) and set of double-pointed (dpn).

Size U.S. 6 (4 mm): 16" and 32" (40 and 80 cm) cir and set of dpn.

Adjust needle size if necessary to obtain the correct gauge.

NOTIONS

Markers (m); tapestry needle.

GAUGE

22 sts and 31 rows = 4" (10 cm) in St st with larger needles.

NOTE

• The tee is meant to be worn with 8–10" (20.5–25.5 cm) of positive ease.

Body

Using smaller cir needle and A, CO 212 (228, 252, 268, 284) sts using the long-tail method (see Glossary). Place marker (pm) and join for working in rnds, being careful not to twist sts.

Rnds 1–6: *K2, p2; rep from * to end of rnd.

Change to longer, larger cir needle.

Set-up rnd: K106 (114, 126, 134, 142), pm, k106 (114, 126, 134, 142).

Knit 24 (26, 26, 28, 30) rnds. Cut A.

Join B and knit 25 (27, 27, 29, 31) rnds. Cut B.

Join C and knit 20 (22, 22, 26, 25) rnds. Piece should measure about 9½ (10¼, 10¼, 11¼, 11¾)" (24 [26, 26, 28.5, 30] cm) from beg.

SHAPE BUST
Sizes 43 (45¾, 51¾)" (109 [116, 131.5] cm) only

Inc rnd: K2, M1R, knit to 2 sts before m, M1L, k2, sl m, k2, M1R, knit to 2 sts before m, M1L, k2—4 sts inc'd.

Knit 3 rnds even.

Next rnd: Rep inc rnd—4 sts inc'd.

Cut C and join D.

Knit 3 rnds even.

Rep Inc rnd on next rnd, then every 4 rnds 0 (1, 1) time(s) more, then every other rnd 3 (2, 4) times—236 (252, 284) sts.

Knit 10 (10, 3) rnds even. Piece should measure about 12¾ (13¾, 13¼)" (32.5 [35, 33.5] cm) from beg.

Next rnd: *Knit to 4 (4, 6) sts before m, BO 8 (8, 12) sts for armhole; rep from * once more—220 (236, 260) sts rem, with 110 (118, 130) sts each for front and back. Set aside.

Size 55¼" (140.5 cm) only

Inc rnd: K2, M1R, knit to 2 sts before m, M1L, k2, sl m, k2, M1R, knit to 2 sts before m, M1L, k2—4 sts inc'd.

Knit 2 rnds even. Cut C and join D.

Knit 1 rnd even.

Rep Inc rnd on next rnd, then every 4 rnds twice more, then every other rnd 5 times—304 sts.

Knit 9 rnds even. Cut D and join E.

Knit 1 rnd. Piece should measure about 15½" (39.5 cm) from beg.

Next rnd: *Knit to 6 sts before m, BO 12 sts for armhole; rep from * once more—280 sts rem, with 140 sts each for front and back. Set aside.

Size 59" (150 cm) only

Inc rnd: K2, M1R, knit to 2 sts before m, M1L, k2, sl m, k2, M1R, knit to 2 sts before m, M1L, k2—4 sts inc'd.

Knit 3 rnds even.

Rep Inc rnd on next rnd—4 sts inc'd.

Knit 1 rnd even.

Cut C and join D.

Knit 2 rnds.

Rep Inc rnd on next rnd, every 4 rnds once more, then every other rnd 6 times—324 sts.

back & front

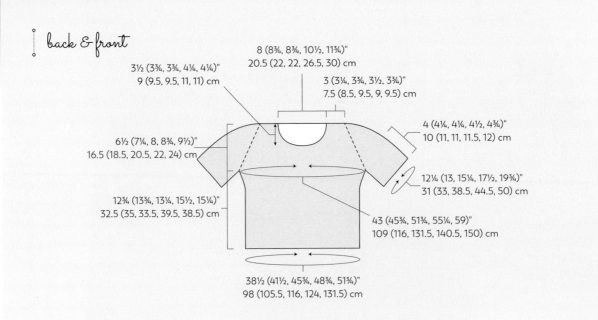

8 (8¾, 8¾, 10½, 11¾)"
20.5 (22, 22, 26.5, 30) cm

3½ (3¾, 3¾, 4¼, 4¼)"
9 (9.5, 9.5, 11, 11) cm

3 (3¼, 3¾, 3½, 3¾)"
7.5 (8.5, 9.5, 9, 9.5) cm

4 (4¼, 4¼, 4½, 4¾)"
10 (11, 11, 11.5, 12) cm

6½ (7¼, 8, 8¾, 9½)"
16.5 (18.5, 20.5, 22, 24) cm

12¼ (13, 15¼, 17½, 19¾)"
31 (33, 38.5, 44.5, 50) cm

12¾ (13¾, 13¼, 15½, 15¼)"
32.5 (35, 33.5, 39.5, 38.5) cm

43 (45¾, 51¾, 55¼, 59)"
109 (116, 131.5, 140.5, 150) cm

38½ (41½, 45¾, 48¾, 51¾)"
98 (105.5, 116, 124, 131.5) cm

Knit 3 rnds even. Piece should measure about 15¼" (38.5 cm) from beg.

Next rnd: *Knit to 8 sts before m, BO 16 sts for armhole; rep from * once more—292 sts rem, with 146 sts each for front and back. Set aside.

Cut D.

Sleeves

Using smaller dpn and C, CO 68 (72, 84, 96, 108) sts using the long-tail method. Pm and join for working in rnds, being careful not to twist sts.

Rnds 1–6: *K2, p2; rep from * to end of rnd.

Change to larger dpn.

Knit 5 (5, 3, 0, 8) rnds. Cut C.

Join D and knit 20 (22, 24, 28, 23) rnds.

Size 55¼" (140.5 cm) only
Cut D and join E.

Knit 1 rnd.

All sizes
Piece should measure 4 (4¼, 4¼, 4½, 4¾)" (10 [11, 11, 11.5, 12] cm) from beg.

Next rnd: Knit to last 4 (4, 6, 6, 8) sts, BO 8 (8, 12, 12, 16) sts—60 (64, 72, 84, 92) sts rem.

Cut yarn and set aside.

Make second sleeve to match, but do not cut yarn.

Yoke

Using longer, larger cir needle, knit 60 (64, 72, 84, 92) sleeve sts with yarn still attached, pm for armhole, knit 110 (118, 130, 140, 146) front sts, pm for armhole, knit rem 60 (64, 72, 84, 92) sleeve sts, pm for armhole, then knit 110 (118, 130, 140, 146) back sts, pm and join for working in rnds—340 (364, 404, 448, 476) sts, with 60 (64, 72, 84, 92) sts for each sleeve, and 110 (118, 130, 140, 146) sts each for front and back.

Knit 1 (1, 1, 1, 2) rnd(s) even.

> **NOTE** *Read through the next sections carefully, as the armholes and sleeve caps are shaped at different rates, while color changes are also being made. The front neck shaping begins while the armhole and sleeve cap shaping are being worked.*

SHAPE ARMHOLES
Armhole dec rnd: K2tog, knit to 2 sts before m, ssk—2 sts dec'd each on front and back.

Rep Armhole dec rnd every other rnd 7 (6, 11, 10, 6) more times, then every 4 rnds 8 (10, 9, 11, 14) times.

At the same time, change to E on 3rd (3rd, 6th, 0, 5th) rnd, then change to F after 25 (27, 27, 29, 31) rnds/rows.

At the same time, when 23 (27, 33, 35, 41) rnds have been worked, shape neck. Pm on center 12 (12, 12, 16, 16) sts of front for neck. Armholes should measure about 3 (3½, 4¼, 4½, 5¼)" (7.5 [9, 11, 11.5, 13.5] cm).

SHAPE NECK

Next rnd: Work to neck marker, BO center 12 (12, 12, 16, 16) sts for neck, work to end of rnd, then work to neck edge.

Beg working back and forth with a WS row and cont armhole and sleeve-cap shaping.

BO 4 sts at beg of next 2 rows, 2 sts at beg of next 6 (8, 8, 10, 12) rows, then dec at each neck edge every RS row 6 (6, 6, 7, 8) times as follows: k1, ssk, work to last 3 sts, k2tog, k1.

SHAPE SLEEVE CAPS
Size 43" (109 cm) only
Dec rnd 1: K2tog, knit to 2 sts before m, ssk—2 sts dec'd.

Rep Dec rnd 1 every other rnd 11 more times, every 4 rnds/rows 2 times, then every RS row 4 times, ending with a WS row—24 sts rem for sleeve cap.

Dec row 2: (RS) K2tog, k4, k2tog, k8, ssk, k4, ssk—20 sts rem for sleeve cap.

Next row and all other WS rows: Purl.

Dec row 3: K2tog, k3, k2tog, k6, ssk, k3, ssk—16 sts rem for sleeve cap.

Dec row 4: K2tog, k2, k2tog, k4, ssk, k2, ssk—12 sts rem for sleeve cap.

Dec row 5: K2tog, k1, k2tog, k2, ssk, k1, ssk—8 sts rem for sleeve cap.

Dec row 6: [K2tog] twice, [ssk] twice—4 sts rem for sleeve cap.

Size 45¾" (116 cm) only
Dec rnd 1: K2tog, knit to 2 sts before m, ssk—2 sts dec'd.

Rep Dec rnd 1 every other rnd 8 more times, every 4 rnds/rows 3 times, then every RS row 8 times—24 sts rem for sleeve cap.

Dec row 2: (RS) K2tog, k4, k2tog, k8, ssk, k4, ssk—20 sts rem for sleeve cap.

Next row and all other WS rows: Purl.

Dec row 3: K2tog, k3, k2tog, k6, ssk, k3, ssk—16 sts rem for sleeve cap.

Dec row 4: K2tog, k2, k2tog, k4, ssk, k2, ssk—12 sts rem for sleeve cap.

Dec row 5: K2tog, k1, k2tog, k2, ssk, k1, ssk—8 sts rem for sleeve cap.

Dec row 6: [K2tog] twice, [ssk] twice—4 sts rem for sleeve cap.

Size 51¾" (131.5 cm) only
Dec rnd 1: K2tog, knit to 2 sts before m, ssk—2 sts dec'd.

Rep Dec rnd 1 every other rnd 11 more times, every 4 rnds/rows 3 times, then every RS row 7 times—28 sts rem for sleeve cap.

Dec row 2: (RS) K2tog, k5, k2tog, k10, ssk, k5, ssk—24 sts rem for sleeve cap.

Next row and all other WS rows: Purl.

Dec row 3: K2tog, k4, k2tog, k8, ssk, k4, ssk—20 sts rem for sleeve cap.

Dec row 4: K2tog, k3, k2tog, k6, ssk, k3, ssk—16 sts rem for sleeve cap.

Dec row 5: K2tog, k2, k2tog, k4, ssk, k2, ssk—12 sts rem for sleeve cap.

Dec row 6: K2tog, k1, k2tog, k2, ssk, k1, ssk—8 sts rem for sleeve cap.

Dec row 7: [K2tog] twice, [ssk] twice—4 sts rem for sleeve cap.

Size 55¼" (140.5 cm) only

Dec rnd 1: K2tog, knit to 2 sts before m, ssk—2 sts dec'd.

Rep Dec rnd 1 every other rnd 11 more times, every 4 rnds/rows 3 times, then every RS row 7 times—40 sts rem for sleeve cap.

Dec row 2: (RS) K2tog, k8, k2tog, k16, ssk, k8, ssk—36 sts rem for sleeve cap.

Next row and all other WS rows: Purl.

Dec row 3: K2tog, k7, k2tog, k14, ssk, k7, ssk—32 sts rem for sleeve cap.

Dec row 4: K2tog, k6, k2tog, k12, ssk, k6, ssk—28 sts rem for sleeve cap.

Dec row 5: K2tog, k5, k2tog, k10, ssk, k5, ssk—24 sts rem for sleeve cap.

Dec row 6: K2tog, k4, k2tog, k8, ssk, k4, ssk—20 sts rem for sleeve cap.

Dec row 7: K2tog, k3, k2tog, k6, ssk, k3, ssk—16 sts rem for sleeve cap.

Dec row 8: K2tog, k2, k2tog, k4, ssk, k2, ssk—12 sts rem for sleeve cap.

Dec row 9: K2tog, k1, k2tog, k2, ssk, k1, ssk—8 sts rem for sleeve cap.

Dec row 10: [K2tog] twice, [ssk] twice—4 sts rem for sleeve cap.

Size 59" (150 cm) only

Work 1 more rnd even over sleeves.

Dec rnd 1: K2tog, k1, k2tog, knit to 5 sts before m, ssk, k1, ssk—4 sts dec'd.

Rep Dec rnd 1 every other rnd 2 more times—80 sts rem for sleeve cap.

Work 1 rnd even.

Dec rnd 2: K2tog, knit to 2 sts before m, ssk—2 sts dec'd.

Rep Dec rnd 2 every other rnd 10 more times, every 4 rnds/rows 4 times, then every RS row 5 times—40 sts rem for sleeve cap.

Dec row 3: (RS) K2tog, k8, k2tog, k16, ssk, k8, ssk—36 sts rem for sleeve cap.

Next row and all other WS rows: Purl.

Dec row 4: K2tog, k7, k2tog, k14, ssk, k7, ssk—32 sts rem for sleeve cap.

Dec row 5: K2tog, k6, k2tog, k12, ssk, k6, ssk—28 sts rem for sleeve cap.

Dec row 6: K2tog, k5, k2tog, k10, ssk, k5, ssk—24 sts rem for sleeve cap.

Dec row 7: K2tog, k4, k2tog, k8, ssk, k4, ssk—20 sts rem for sleeve cap.

Dec row 8: K2tog, k3, k2tog, k6, ssk, k3, ssk—16 sts rem for sleeve cap.

Dec row 9: K2tog, k2, k2tog, k4, ssk, k2, ssk—12 sts rem for sleeve cap.

Dec row 10: K2tog, k1, k2tog, k2, ssk, k1, ssk—8 sts rem for sleeve cap.

Dec row 11: [K2tog] twice, [ssk] twice—4 sts rem for sleeve cap.

All sizes

When all shaping is complete, 120 (128, 136, 142, 152) sts rem, with 4 sts for each sleeve, 17 (18, 20, 19, 20) sts for each front, and 78 (84, 88, 96, 104) sts for back. Armholes should measure 6½ (7¼, 8, 8¾, 9½)" (16.5 [18.5, 20.5, 22, 24] cm).

JOIN SHOULDERS

Next row: (WS) Purl to m, remove m, p2. Fold work with RS tog and needle tips facing in same direction. Using dpn, join 19 (20, 22, 21, 22) sts using three-needle BO (see Glossary), purl to next m, remove m, p2, fold work with RS tog and needle tips facing in same direction. Join 19 (20, 22, 21, 22) sts using three-needle BO—44 (48, 48, 58, 64) sts rem for back neck.

NECKBAND

Cut F.

Next row: (RS) With shorter smaller cir needle and A, knit rem 44 (48, 48, 58, 64) back neck sts, pick up and knit 72 (76, 76, 86, 92) sts evenly spaced along front neck, pm and join for working in rnds—116 (124, 124, 144, 156) sts.

Rnds 1–6: *K2, p2; rep from * around.

BO all loosely in ribbing.

Finishing

Weave in ends. Sew underarm seams. Block to measurements.

MIXED-MEDIA *socks*

These comfy socks are knit from the top down using an intarsia-in-the-round technique to create a color block on one half and a more subtle gradient on the other half that slowly melts from one color to another. The clean lines and classic reverse stockinette stitch showcase the variegated and speckled yarns. German short-rows require no wrapping for easy shaping. • **Mara Catherine Bryner**

FINISHED SIZES
5¾ (6¾, 7¾, 8¾)"
(14.5 [17, 19.5, 22] cm)
foot circumference.

Shown in size 6¾"
(17 cm). Socks are
intended to be worn
with ½" (1.3 cm)
negative ease.

YARN
Fingering weight
(#1 Super Fine).

Shown here: Machete
Shoppe Simple Sock
(75% superwash
merino wool, 25%
nylon; 463 yd [423
m]/ 3½ oz [100 g]):
Rooster (pink, A),
1 skein; Purrmaid
(purple, B), 1 skein;
Blue Bell (dark blue,
C), 1 skein; Dang
Girl! (light blue, D), 1
skein; Drugwolf (white
speckled, E), 1 skein.

NEEDLES
Size U.S. 1 (2.25 mm):
set of 5 double-
pointed (dpn), 2
circular (cir), or 1
long cir, as you
prefer for small-
circumference knitting.

*Adjust needle size if
necessary to achieve
the correct gauge.*

NOTIONS
Markers (m); stitch
holder or waste yarn;
tapestry needle;
sock blocker.

GAUGE
32 sts and 50 rnds =
4" (10 cm) in St st.

NOTE
• To make these socks
more accessible and
easier to knit, they
are worked inside out
(knit side facing).

STITCH GUIDE

German Short-rows

Unlike traditional wrap-and-turn short-rows, German short-rows require no wrapping. In this short-row method, you work to the desired turning point, then turn the work and create a double stitch (DS). A double stitch is created by bringing your working yarn over the needle from front to back and pulling it taut so that the stitch below the needle is pulled up over the needle, resulting in two legs on the needle (this double stitch still counts as one stitch). German short-rows are easy to work and create a clean, finished look.

Making a Double Stitch (DS) on a Knit Row/Rnd

Step 1: Knit to desired turning point and turn work.

Step 2: Slip first st on LH needle (last st worked before turning) pwise wyf.

Step 3: Bring yarn over RH needle and to back of work, pull it until the two legs of the st below are wrapped over needle.* This is the double stitch.

Step 4: Bring yarn between needles to front of work to begin next row.

Making a Double Stitch (DS) on a Purl Row/Rnd

Step 1: Purl to desired turning point and turn work.

Step 2: Bring yarn between needles to front of work.

Step 3: Slip first st on LH needle (last st worked before turning) pwise wyf.

Step 4: Bring yarn over RH needle and to back of work and pull it until the two legs of the st below are wrapped over needle. This is the double stitch.

NOTE *If you do not pull tightly enough when creating the DS, gaps can occur. Make sure to tighten your tension when making the DS and knitting or purling the DS later.*

Working a DS on a knit row/rnd:

Knit to DS, insert RH needle kwise into both front legs of DS, knit both legs together as one st.

Working a DS on a purl row/rnd:

Purl to DS, insert RH needle pwise into both front legs of DS, purl both legs together as one st.

Cuff

With A, CO 48 (56, 64, 72) sts using the knitted method (see Glossary). Place marker (pm) and join for working in rnds, being careful not to twist sts.

Purl 9 rnds.

Inc rnd: P12 (14, 16, 18), M1, p24 (28, 32, 36), M1, purl to end of rnd—50 (58, 66, 74) sts.

Next rnd: [P1, k11 (13, 15, 17)] twice, [p1, k12 (14, 16, 18)] twice.

Next rnd: [Sl 1 wyf, k11 (13, 15, 17)] twice, [sl 1 wyf, k12 (14, 16, 18)] twice.

Rep last 2 rnds 7 (7, 11, 11) more times.

Leg
BEGIN GRADIENT STRIPING PATTERN

NOTE *Remember to make all color changes on the WS (knit side) of the sock.*

Section One

Rnds 1 and 2: With A, p1, k11 (13, 15, 17), p1, join B, k11 (13, 15, 17), p1, k12 (14, 16, 18), p1, turn, DS, p12 (14, 16, 18), sl 1 wyb, p11 (13, 15, 17), sl 1 wyb, change to A and interlock yarns, p11 (13, 15, 17), sl 1 wyb, p12 (14, 16, 18), knit the DS, turn, sl 1 wyb, k12 (14, 16, 18).

Rnd 3: With A, [p1, k11 (13, 15, 17)] twice, [p1, k12 (14, 16, 18)] twice.

Rnd 4: With A, [sl 1 wyf, k11 (13, 15, 17)] twice, [sl 1 wyf, k12 (14, 16, 18)] twice.

Rep last 4 rnds 1 (1, 2, 2) more time(s).

Section Two
Rnd 1: With A, p1, k11 (13, 15, 17), p1, change to B, k11 (13, 15, 17), [p1, k12 (14, 16, 18)] twice.

Rnd 2: With B, [sl 1 wyf, k11 (13, 15, 17)] twice, [sl 1 wyf, k12 (14, 16, 18)] twice.

Rnds 3 and 4: With B, p1, k11 (13, 15, 17), p1, change to A, k11 (13, 15, 17), p1, k12 (14, 16, 18), p1, turn, DS, p12 (14, 16, 18), sl 1 wyb, p11 (13, 15, 17), sl 1 wyb, change to B, p11 (13, 15, 17), sl 1 wyb, p12 (14, 16, 18), knit the DS, turn, sl 1 wyf, k12 (14, 16, 18).

Rnd 5: With B, [p1, k11 (13, 15, 17)] twice, [p1, k12 (14, 16, 18)] twice.

Rnd 6: With B, [sl 1 wyf, k11 (13, 15, 17)] twice, [sl 1 wyf, k12 (14, 16, 18)] twice.

Rnds 7 and 8: With B, p1, k11 (13, 15, 17), p1, change to A, k11 (13, 15, 17), p1, k12 (14, 16, 18), p1, turn, DS, p12 (14, 16, 18), sl 1 wyb, p11 (13, 15, 17), sl 1 wyb, change to B, p11 (13, 15, 17), sl 1 wyb, p12 (14, 16, 18), knit DS, turn, sl 1 wyf, k12 (14, 16, 18).

Rep last 4 rnds 0 (0, 1, 1) more time(s). Cut A.

Work 1 rnd even. Piece should measure about 3½ (3½, 4¾, 4¾)" (9 [9, 12, 12] cm) from beg.

Heel
Set-up row: With B, [sl 1 wyf, k11 (13, 15, 17)] twice, sl 1 wyf, place these 25 (29, 33, 37) sts onto holder or waste yarn—25 (29, 33, 37) sts rem.

FIRST HALF OF HEEL
Row 1: K12 (14, 16, 18), sl 1 wyf, knit to end of row, turn.

Row 2: DS, p11 (13, 15, 17), k1, purl to end of row, turn.

Row 3: DS, work in est patt to DS, turn.

Rep last row 14 (18, 30, 22) more times—9 (9, 11, 13) sts rem in work at center of heel.

CENTER OF HEEL
Row 1: Work to end of row, working each DS as you come to it.

Row 2: Work to end of row, working rem DS as you come to them.

Row 3: [Sl 1 wyf, k11 (13, 15, 17)] twice, sl 1 wyf.

SECOND HALF OF HEEL

Row 1: Work 18 (20, 23, 26) sts, turn.

Row 2: DS, work 11 (11, 13, 15) sts, turn.

Row 3: DS, work to 1 st past DS, turn.

Row 4: DS, work to 1 st past DS, turn.

Rep last 2 rows until all sts are back in work and 1 DS rem at each end of heel sts.

Foot

Return held 25 (29, 33, 37) sts to needles—50 (58, 66, 74) sts. Join and work in rnds again.

Rnd 1: Work to end of heel sts, working all DS as you come to them.

Rnd 2: [P1, k11 (13, 15, 17)] twice, [p1, k12 (14, 16, 18)] twice.

Rnd 3: [Sl 1 wyf, k11 (13, 15, 17)] twice, [sl 1 wyf, k12 (14, 16, 18)] twice.

*Join C. With B and C, rep Rnds 1–4 of Section One 2 (2, 3, 3) times.

Rep Rnds 1–8 of Section Two once, then Rnds 5–8 zero (0, 1, 1) more time(s).

With C only, rep Rnds 5 and 6 of Section Two 3 times.*

Cut B, and join D. Rep from * to * once, working with C and D.

Cut C, and join E. Rep from * to * once, working with D and E. Cut D. Foot should measure about 6¾ (7, 9¼, 9½)" (17 [18, 23.5, 24] cm) from heel.

Cont even if necessary until foot measures 1½ (1½, 1¾, 2)" (3.8 [3.8, 4.5, 5] cm) less than desired length. Pm at center of row.

Toe

Rnd 1: (dec) *P1, ssk, work 1 to 3 sts before m, k2tog, p1; rep from * once more—4 sts dec'd.

Rnd 2: Work even.

Rep Rnds 1 and 2 five (6, 7, 8) more times—26 (30, 34, 38) sts rem.

Divide sts evenly over 2 needles, with 13 (15, 17, 19) sts on each needle. Join toe using Kitchener st (see Glossary).

Finishing

Weave in ends. Turn sock so RS is facing. Block using sock blocker.

SNOW MELT *cowl*

This coolly elegant cowl celebrates winter at its best! A cool-colored gradient and lace stitch pattern echo silent icy landscapes, while soft merino wool keeps you warm whenever the temperature drops. It's constructed to mimic a triangular shawl, so you can enjoy both the comfort of a cowl and the beauty of a shawl. • **Stella Egidi**

FINISHED SIZE

About 18½" (47 cm) neck circumference, 39½" (100.5 cm) bottom circumference, 18¼" (46.5 cm) front length, and 8¾" (22 cm) back length.

YARN

Fingering weight (#1 Super Fine).

Shown here: Freia Fibers Ombré Merino Fingering Shawl Ball (100% merino wool; 430 yd [393 m]/3½ oz [100 g]): Ice Queen, 1 ball.

NEEDLES

Size U.S. 3 (3.25 mm): 24" (60 cm) circular (cir).

Adjust needle size if necessary to obtain the correct gauge.

NOTIONS

Markers (m); tapestry needle.

GAUGE

24 sts and 48 rows = 4" (10 cm) in Garter st.

NOTES

• The cowl begins flat with a garter tab, then increases four stitches (one at each edge and one at each side of the central vertical line) every RS row.

• The edges are then joined and the cowl is worked in the round with only two increases every other round (one at each side of the central vertical line). The bottom garter edge is worked in the round with no more increases and finished with a picot bind-off.

Cowl

GARTER TAB

CO 2 sts. Do not join. Work 3 rows in Garter st (knit every row).

Next row: K2, rotate piece 90 degrees to the right, pick up and knit 2 sts along side edge (1 st in each garter ridge), rotate piece 90 degrees to the right, pick up and knit 2 sts in CO edge—6 sts.

Set-up row 1: [K2, yo] twice, k2—8 sts.

Set-up row 2: K2, yo, k1, place marker (pm), k2, pm, k1, yo, k2—10 sts.

FIRST GARTER SECTION

Row 1: (RS) K2, yo, knit to m, ayo (see Stitch Guide), sl m, k2, sl m, ayo, knit to last 2 sts, yo, k2—4 sts inc'd.

Row 2: (WS) Knit to m, sl m, p2, sl m, knit to end of row.

Rep last 2 rows 35 more times—154 sts.

Joining rnd: K1f&b, knit to m, ayo, sl m, k2, sl m, ayo, knit to last st, sl 1, knit first st of rnd, psso, pm and join for working in rnds—156 sts.

Next rnd: Knit, slipping m when you come to them.

FIRST LACE SECTION

Set-up rnd: Working Rnd 1 of Chart A, beg at right edge of chart, work first st, rep next 9 sts 8 times, k2, yo, k1, yo, sl m, k2, sl m, yo, k1, yo, k2, rep next 9 sts to last 2 sts, ssk—2 sts inc'd.

Work Rnds 2–24 of Chart A in established patt—180 sts.

SECOND GARTER SECTION

Rnd 1: (inc) Knit to marker, ayo, sl m, k2, sl m, ayo, knit to end of rnd—2 sts inc'd.

Rnd 2: Purl to marker, sl m, k2, sl m, purl to end of rnd.

Rep Rnds 1 and 2 eight more times, then rep Rnd 1 once more—200 sts.

Next row: Knit.

knit	ssk
yo	ayo (see Stitch Guide)
k2tog	pattern repeat

CHART A

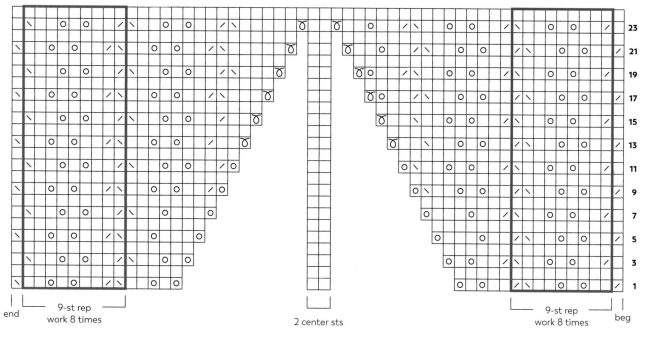

SECOND LACE SECTION

Set-up rnd: Working Rnd 1 of Chart B, beg at right edge of chart, work first 9 sts, rep next 9 sts 10 times, ayo, sl m, k2, sl m, ayo, rep next 9 sts 10 times, then work 9 sts at left edge of chart—2 sts inc'd.

Work Rnds 2–24 of Chart B in established patt—224 sts.

BOTTOM EDGE

Rnd 1: Knit.

Rnd 2: Purl.

Rep Rnds 1 and 2 five more times.

Picot Bind-off

Bind off as foll: BO 4 sts, *CO 2 using the knitted method (see Glossary), BO 6 sts; rep from * to end of rnd.

Finishing

Weave in ends. Block to measurements.

	knit
o	yo
∕	k2tog
∖	ssk
୪	ayo (see Stitch Guide)
⬜	pattern repeat

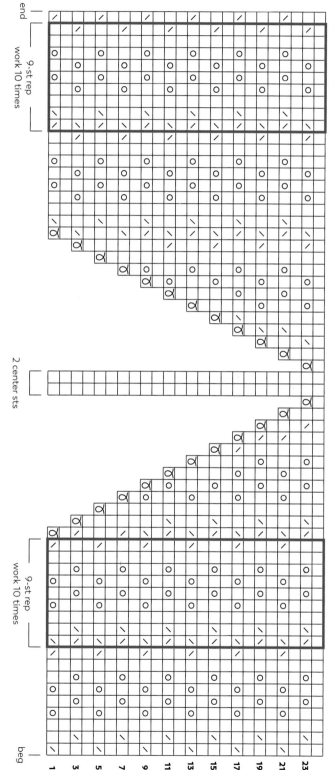

CHART B

COLOR-BLOCK *mittens*

These fast and fun mittens feature three luscious shades of purple. Two strands are held double throughout; one strand is swapped for each wide stripe to create a bold gradient effect. The long cuffs feature a satisfying reversible slip-stitch rib—wear them long, scrunch them up, or fold them over depending on your coat or mood. • **Meghan Babin**

FINISHED SIZE

About 7¼" (18.5 cm) hand circumference and 14" (35.5 cm) long.

YARN

Fingering weight (#1 Super Fine).

Shown here: Brooklyn Tweed Loft (100% Wyoming-grown Targhee-Columbia wool; 275 yd [252 m] 1¾ oz [50 g]): Postcard (A), 1 ball; Blanket Fort (B), 1 ball; Plume (C), 1 ball.

NEEDLES

Size U.S. 5 (3.75 mm): circular (cir) or double-pointed (dpn) for preferred method of circular knitting.

Adjust needle size if necessary to obtain the correct gauge.

NOTIONS

Markers (m); waste yarn; tapestry needle.

GAUGE

20 sts and 34 rnds = 4" (10 cm) in St st.

20 sts and 46 rnds = 4" (10 cm) in Slipped Garter Rib.

NOTES

• Mittens are worked in the round from the bottom up.

• These mittens are worked using two strands of yarn held together throughout. One strand of yarn is changed every 24 rounds to create the gradient effect.

• When working with two strands of the same color, use the end from the center of the ball and the end from the outside of the ball.

STITCH GUIDE

Slipped Garter Rib (multiple of 4 sts)

Rnd 1: *Sl 1 wyb, p3; rep from * to end of rnd.

Rnd 2: K2, *sl 1 wyf, k3; rep from * to last 2 sts, sl 1 wyf, k1.

Rep Rnds 1 and 2 for patt.

Mittens

CUFF

Holding 2 strands of A tog, CO 36 sts. Place marker (pm) and join for working in rnds, being careful not to twist sts.

Work in slipped garter rib (see Stitch Guide) for 24 rnds.

Break 1 strand of A and join 1 strand of B. Cont in Slipped Garter Rib for 24 rnds.

Break strand of A and join second strand of B. Cont in Slipped Garter Rib for 24 rnds.

Break 1 strand of B and join 1 strand of C.

HAND

Work in St st (knit every rnd) for 6 rnds.

Right Thumb Gusset

Inc rnd 1: K4, pm, M1R, k1, M1L, pm, knit to end of rnd—2 sts inc'd.

Next 2 rnds: Knit.

Inc rnd 2: K4, sl m, M1R, knit to m, M1L, sl m, knit to end of rnd—2 sts inc'd.

Rep last 3 rnds 4 more times—48 sts, with 13 sts between m for gusset.

Work 2 rnds even. Break strand of B and join second strand of C.

Next rnd: K4, remove m, place next 13 sts onto waste yarn for thumb, using the backward-loop method (see Glossary), CO 1 st over gap, remove m, knit to end of rnd—36 sts rem.

Left Thumb Gusset

Inc rnd 1: K14, pm, M1R, k1, M1L, pm, knit to end of rnd—2 sts inc'd.

Next 2 rnds: Knit.

Inc rnd 2: K14, sl m, M1R, knit to m, M1L, sl m, knit to end of rnd—2 sts inc'd.

Rep last 3 rnds 4 more times—48 sts, with 13 sts between m for gusset.

Work 2 rnds even. Break strand of B and join second strand of C.

Next rnd: K14, remove m, place next 13 sts onto waste yarn for thumb, using the backward-loop method, CO 1 st over gap, remove m, knit to end of rnd—36 sts rem.

UPPER HAND

Work even in St st for 23 rnds more. Break 1 strand of C and join 1 strand of B.

Work even until piece measures 13" (33 cm), or 1" (2.5 cm) less than desired length.

Shape Tip

Rnd 1: (dec) *Ssk, k5, k2tog, pm; rep from * 3 more times—8 sts dec'd.

Rnd 2: Knit.

Rnd 3: (dec) *Ssk, knit to 2 sts before m, k2tog, sl m; rep from * 3 more times—8 sts dec'd.

Rnds 4–6: Rep Rnds 2 and 3 once, then rep Rnd 2 once more, and remove m on last rnd—12 sts rem.

Rnd 7: (dec) *Ssk, k2, k2tog; rep from * once more—8 sts rem.

Rnd 8: (dec) *K2tog; rep from * around—4 sts rem.

Cut yarn, leaving a 6" (15 cm) tail, thread tail through rem sts and pull tightly to close hole, and fasten off on WS.

THUMB

Return held 13 sts to needle, pick up and knit 3 sts in gap at top of opening—16 sts. Distribute sts evenly over needle(s). Pm and join for working in rnds. Join 2 strands of C.

Rnd 1: (dec) Knit to last 4 sts, k2tog, k1, sl 1—15 sts rem.

Rnd 2: (dec) K2tog, knit to end of rnd—14 sts rem.

Next rnd: Knit.

Cont even in St st until thumb measures ¼" (0.6 cm) less than desired length.

Shape Tip

Dec rnd 1: *K2tog, k1; rep from * to last 2 sts, k2tog—9 sts rem.

Dec rnd 2: *K2tog; rep from * to last st, k1—5 sts rem.

Cut yarn, leaving a 6" (15 cm) tail, thread tail through rem sts, and pull tightly to close hole, and fasten off on WS.

Finishing

Weave in ends. Wet-block to finished measurements.

LACY STRIPES *shawl*

This asymmetrical triangular shawl starts with just three stitches and grows to a beautiful lace border. The lace-insert and border patterns are easy to memorize and give a striking effect with the smooth shifting of the different gradient colors. The bold cherry yarn contrasts with the cool gray-blue gradient yarns. • **Sara Maternini—La Cave à Laine**

FINISHED SIZE
About 84" (213.5 cm) wide and 38" (96.5 cm) deep.

YARN
Fingering weight (#1 Super Fine).

Shown here: SnailYarn Merino Single (100% superwash merino wool; 400 yd [366 m]/3½ oz [100 g]): Cherry (A), 1 hank.

SnailYarn Merino Single Gradient Set (100% superwash merino wool; 400 yd [366 m]/3½ oz [100 g]): Slate, 1 set; label colors B (lightest) to F (darkest).

NEEDLES
Size U.S. 6 (4 mm).

Size U.S. 8 (5 mm): straight or double-pointed (dpn) for bind-off.

Adjust needle sizes if necessary to obtain the correct gauge.

NOTIONS
Tapestry needle.

GAUGE
22 sts and 49 rows = 4" (10 cm) in Garter st with larger needles.

NOTES
• When working the lace inserts do not cut Color A, but pass it over the working yarn along the right edge to form a pleasant selvedge.

• Slip-stitches purlwise unless otherwise noted.

STITCH GUIDE

Simple Mesh Lace A (multiple of 2 sts)

Row 1: (RS) K1, k1f&b, *yo, ssk; rep from * to last 2 sts, k1, sl 1 wyf.

Row 2: (WS) K1, k2tog, k1, *yo, ssk; rep from * to last st, yo, sl 1 wyf.

Row 3: K1, k1f&b, *yo, ssk; rep from * to last st, sl 1 wyf.

Row 4: K1, k2tog, *yo, ssk; rep from * to last st, yo, sl 1 wyf.

Simple Mesh Lace B (multiple of 2 sts)

Row 1: (RS) K1, k1f&b, *yo, k2tog; rep from * to last 2 sts, k1, sl 1 wyf.

Row 2: (WS) K1, k2tog, k1, *yo, k2tog; rep from * to last st, yo, sl 1 wyf.

Row 3: K1, k1f&b, *yo, k2tog; rep from * to last st, sl 1 wyf.

Row 4: K1, k2tog, *yo, k2tog; rep from * to last st, yo, sl 1 wyf.

Border Lace (multiple of 6 sts + 4)

Row 1 and all other WS rows: K1, purl to last st, sl 1 wyf.

Row 2: (RS) K2, *yo, ssk, k1, k2tog, yo, k1; rep from * to last 2 sts, k1, sl 1 wyf.

Row 4: K2, *yo, k1, sk2p, k1, yo, k1; rep from * to last 2 sts, k1, sl 1 wyf.

Row 6: K2, *k2tog, yo, k1, yo, ssk, k1; rep from * to last 2 sts, k1, sl 1 wyf.

Row 8: K1, k2tog, *[k1, yo] twice, k1, sk2p; rep from * to last 7 sts, [k1, yo] twice, k1, ssk, k1, sl 1 wyf.

Rep Rows 1–8 for patt.

Shawl

With A, CO 3 sts.

Foundation row: (WS) K2, yo, sl 1 wyf—4 sts.

Row 1: (RS) K1, k1f&b, knit to last st, sl 1 wyf—1 st inc'd.

Row 2: (WS) K1, k2tog, knit to last st, yo, sl 1 wyf.

Rep last 2 rows 125 more times, ending with a WS row—130 sts.

LACE INSERT 1

Join B and work Rows 1–4 of simple mesh lace A (see Stitch Guide or chart)—132 sts. Cut B.

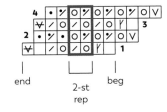

SIMPLE MESH LACE A

SIMPLE MESH LACE B

BORDER LACE

| | k on RS, p on WS
| • | p on RS, k on WS
| o | yo
| / | k2tog on RS
| ⅄ | k2tog on WS
| \ | ssk on RS
| ↘ | ssk on WS
| ⋀ | sk2p (see Glossary)
| V | sl 1 wyf on WS
| ⅄ | sl 1 wyf on RS
| Γ | k1f&b (see Glossary)
| | end last rep ssk
| | pattern repeat

GARTER BAND

Row 1: (RS) With A, k1, k1f&b, knit
to last st, sl 1 wyf—1 st inc'd.

Row 2: (WS) K1, k2tog, knit
to last st, yo, sl 1 wyf.

Rep last 2 rows 3 more times—136 sts.

LACE INSERT 2

Join C and work Rows 1–4 of simple
mesh lace A—138 sts. Cut C.

GARTER BAND

Row 1: (RS) With A, k1, k1f&b, knit
to last st, sl 1 wyf—1 st inc'd.

Row 2: (WS) K1, k2tog, knit
to last st, yo, sl 1 wyf.

Rep last 2 rows 3 more times—142 sts.

LACE INSERT 3

Join D and work Rows 1–4 of simple mesh lace A—144 sts. Cut D.

GARTER BAND

Row 1: (RS) With A, k1, k1f&b, knit to last st, sl 1 wyf—1 st inc'd.

Row 2: (WS) K1, k2tog, knit to last st, yo, sl 1 wyf.

Rep last 2 rows 3 more times—148 sts.

LACE INSERT 4

Join E and work Rows 1–4 of simple mesh lace A—150 sts. Cut E.

GARTER BAND

Row 1: (RS) With A, k1, k1f&b, knit to last st, sl 1 wyf—1 st inc'd.

Row 2: (WS) K1, k2tog, knit to last st, yo, sl 1 wyf.

Rep last 2 rows 3 more times—154 sts. Cut A.

LACE INSERT 5

Join E and work Rows 1–4 of simple mesh lace B (see Stitch Guide or chart) 3 times—160 sts. Cut E.

Join D and work Rows 1–4 of simple mesh lace B twice, then rep Rows 1 and 2 once more—165 sts. Cut D.

Join C and work Rows 3 and 4 of simple mesh lace B, work Rows 1–4 once, then rep Rows 1 and 2 once more—169 sts. Cut C.

Join B and work Rows 1–4 of simple mesh lace B once, then rep Rows 1 and 2 once more—172 sts. Cut B.

BORDER

Join F and knit 1 row.

Next row: (WS) Working Row 1 of border lace (see Stitch Guide or chart), beg at left edge of chart and work first 2 sts, rep next 6 sts 28 times, then work 2 sts at right edge of chart.

Next row: (RS) Working Row 2 of border lace, beg at right edge of chart and work first 2 sts, rep next 6 sts 28 times, then work 2 sts at left edge of chart.

Work Rows 3–8 of chart once, rep Rows 1–8 again, then rep Rows 1–5 once more.

BO all sts loosely using bigger needle and Jeny's Surprisingly Stretchy BO (see Glossary).

Finishing

Weave in ends but do not trim until after piece has been blocked.

Wet-block to measurements, pinning out all points along border edge and being careful to open up the yarnovers. Trim ends.

SEED-STITCH *pullover*

This easygoing sweater is knit entirely in seed stitch from the top down and features a graceful boat neckline and three-quarter-length sleeves. Five shades of purple blend perfectly for a gradient that is bold yet sophisticated. Increasing the needle size as the body is worked gives the pullover a gentle, flattering A-line shape without having to work any shaping! • **Toby Roxane Barna**

FINISHED SIZES

34½ (39¼, 43¼, 48, 52, 56¼, 61)" (87.5 [99.5, 110, 122, 132, 143, 155] cm) bust circumference and 19 (20¼, 20¾, 21½, 22, 23¾, 23¾)" (48.5 [51.5, 52.5, 54.5, 56, 60.5, 60.5] cm) long from neck edge.

Pullover shown measures 39¼" (99.5 cm).

YARN

Worsted weight (#4 Medium).

Shown here: June Pryce Fiber Arts Greenwich Worsted (100% superwash merino wool; 218 yd [199 m]/3½ oz [100 g]): Just a Whiff (A), 1 (1, 2, 2, 2, 3, 3) skein(s); Shrinking Violet (B), 1 (1, 2, 2, 2, 3, 3) skein(s); Bring It On! (C), 1 (1, 2, 2, 2, 3, 3) skein(s); Séance (D), 1 (1, 2, 2, 2, 3, 3) skein(s); Witchy Woman (E), 1 (1, 2, 2, 2, 3, 3) skein(s).

NEEDLES

Size U.S. 7 (4.5 mm): 16" and 24" (40 and 60 cm) circular (cir) and set of double-pointed (dpn).

Size U.S. 8 (5 mm): 24" (60 cm) cir and set of dpn.

Size U.S. 9 (5.5 mm): 24" (60 cm) cir and set of dpn.

Size U.S. 10 (6 mm): 24" (60 cm) cir and set of dpn.

Size U.S. 10½ (6.5 mm): 24" (60 cm) cir.

Size U.S. 11 (8 mm): 24" (60 cm) cir.

Adjust needle size if necessary to obtain the correct gauge.

NOTIONS

Markers (m); waste yarn; tapestry needle.

GAUGE

20 sts and 36 rnds = 4" (10 cm) in Seed st with size 7 (4.5 mm) needles.

18½ sts and 33 rnds = 4" (10 cm) in Seed st with size 8 (5 mm) needles.

NOTES

• This sweater is worked in the round from the top down.

• Sleeve stitches are placed on holders while body is worked, then sleeve stitches are picked up and knit toward cuff.

Yoke

Using shorter size U.S. 7 (4.5 mm) cir needle and A, CO 136 (122, 124, 118, 116, 108, 126) sts. Place marker (pm) and join for working in rnds, being careful not to twist sts.

> **NOTE** *Change to longer circular needle when there are too many sts to work comfortably on the shorter needle.*

Set-up rnd: K22 (15, 14, 11, 8, 4, 9), pm, k46 (46, 48, 48, 50, 50, 54), pm, k22 (15, 14, 11, 8, 4, 9), pm, knit to end of rnd.

Inc rnd: [K1, M1R, work in Seed st to 1 st before m, M1L, k1, sl m] 4 times—8 sts inc'd.

Next rnd: [K1, work in Seed st to 1 st before m, k1] 4 times.

Cont in established patt, rep Inc rnd every 4 (3, 3, 3, 3, 3) rnds 8 (2, 9, 18, 22, 30) times, then every 5 (4, 4, 4, 4, 0) rnds 3 (13,

9, 4, 2, 6, 0) times—232 (250, 276, 302, 316, 340, 374) sts, with 70 (78, 86, 94, 100, 108, 116) sts each for front and back, and 46 (47, 52, 57, 58, 62, 71) sts for each sleeve. Piece should measure about 5½ (6¾, 7¼, 8, 8½, 10¼, 10¼)" (14 [17, 18.5, 20.5, 21.5, 26, 26] cm) from CO edge.

At the same time, change to next darker color every 4" (10 cm).

DIVIDE FOR BODY AND SLEEVES

Next rnd: Sl 46 (47, 52, 57, 58, 62, 71) sleeve sts onto waste yarn, remove m, turn work and CO 10 (13, 14, 17, 20, 22, 25) sts for underarm using the cable method (see Glossary), work to m, remove m, sl next 46 (47, 52, 57, 58, 62, 71) sleeve sts onto waste yarn, CO 10 (13, 14, 17, 20, 22, 25) sts for underarm, remove m, then work to end of rnd—160 (182, 200, 222, 240, 260, 282) sts.

> **NOTE** *One marker remains for beginning of round.*

Body

Change to size U.S. 8 (5 mm) cir needle.

Cont even in Seed st, changing to next larger cir needle every 2¾" (7 cm) until piece measures 13½" (34.5 cm) from bottom of armhole.

BO all sts in patt.

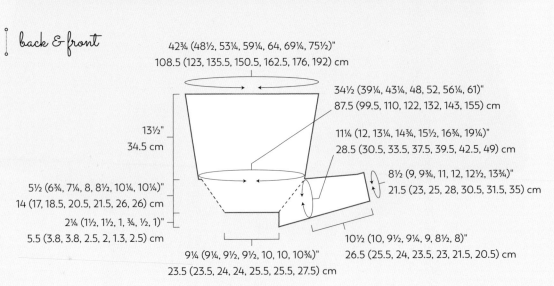

back & front

42¾ (48½, 53¼, 59¼, 64, 69¼, 75½)"
108.5 (123, 135.5, 150.5, 162.5, 176, 192) cm

34½ (39¼, 43¼, 48, 52, 56¼, 61)"
87.5 (99.5, 110, 122, 132, 143, 155) cm

13½"
34.5 cm

11¼ (12, 13¼, 14¾, 15½, 16¾, 19¼)"
28.5 (30.5, 33.5, 37.5, 39.5, 42.5, 49) cm

8½ (9, 9¾, 11, 12, 12½, 13¾)"
21.5 (23, 25, 28, 30.5, 31.5, 35) cm

5½ (6¾, 7¼, 8, 8½, 10¼, 10¼)"
14 (17, 18.5, 20.5, 21.5, 26, 26) cm

2¼ (1½, 1½, 1, ¾, ½, 1)"
5.5 (3.8, 3.8, 2.5, 2, 1.3, 2.5) cm

9¼ (9¼, 9½, 9½, 10, 10, 10¾)"
23.5 (23.5, 24, 24, 25.5, 25.5, 27.5) cm

10½ (10, 9½, 9¼, 9, 8½, 8)"
26.5 (25.5, 24, 23.5, 23, 21.5, 20.5) cm

Sleeves

> **NOTE** *Divide remaining yarn of each color in half (you may want to weigh it) and use half for each sleeve. The length of your sleeves may vary from the pattern, depending on how much yarn is left over for each.*

Return held 46 (47, 52, 57, 58, 62, 71) sleeve sts to size U.S. 7 (4.5 mm) dpns. With B and RS facing, beg at center of underarm CO, pick up and knit 5 (7, 7, 9, 10, 11, 13) sts, work in established patt over sleeve sts, then pick up and knit 5 (6, 7, 8, 10, 11, 12) sts along rem CO edge—56 (60, 66, 74, 78, 84, 96) sts. Pm and join for working in rnds.

Work 3 rnds even in established patt.

Dec rnd: Work in Seed st to next knit st (2 or 3 sts), sk2p, then work to end of rnd—2 sts dec'd.

Rep Dec rnd every 8 (6, 6, 5, 5, 4, 3) rnds 8 (9, 10, 11, 11, 13, 16) times—38 (40, 44, 50, 54, 56, 62) sts rem. At the same time, change to next color when you run out of half of each rem color and change to next larger dpns each time you change colors.

Cont even until sleeve measures about 10½ (10, 9½, 9¼, 9, 8½, 8)" (26.5 [25.5, 24, 23.5, 23, 21.5, 20.5] cm), or until 1½ (1½, 1¾, 2, 2¼, 2¼, 2½) yd (1.4 [1.4, 1.6, 1.8, 2, 2, 2.3] m) of darkest color rem. BO all sts in pattern.

Finishing

Weave in ends. Block to measurements.

FLAME LACE *shawl*

Knit from a single ball of yarn that travels the color spectrum from reddish-purple to yellow to off white, this half-circle shawl features a chevron pattern reminiscent of flames. The flames grow wider and longer with each lace segment worked and showcase the beauty of the yarn changing colors at long intervals. • **Mone Dräger**

FINISHED SIZE

About 60" (152.5 cm) wide and 27" (68.5 cm) long.

YARN

Fingering weight (#1 Super Fine).

Shown here: Twisted Fiber Art Arial Evolution Extra Large (100% superwash merino wool; 1,020 yd [933 m]/7½ oz [210 g]): Eclipse, 1 ball.

NEEDLES

Size U.S. 3 (3.25 mm): 40" (100 cm) circular (cir) to accommodate the large number of stitches.

Adjust needle size if necessary to achieve the correct gauge.

NOTIONS

Tapestry needle.

GAUGE

22 sts and 30 rows = 4" (10 cm) in Flame patt 2.

NOTES

• The shawl is designed to show the complete color scheme and uses almost all of the yarn. To avoid running out of yarn, when working the final lace section, weigh the yarn after completing Row 60. There should be about 2 oz (56.5 g) left (1½ oz [42.5 g] to complete this lace section; ½ oz [14 g] for the edging). If there is not sufficient yarn, continue with the edging instructions.

• Read all charts from bottom to top and each row from right to left. WS rows are not shown in the charts. Work all WS rows as follows: Sl 2 wyf, purl to last 2 sts, sl 2 wyf.

• The edging is shaped using German short-rows with double stitches (DS).

STITCH GUIDE

Double Stitch (DS)

Bring the working yarn in front, slip the next stitch purlwise, bring the working yarn from front to back over the needle and pull on it enough to bring the legs of that stitch over the needle. The stitch on the needle looks like a double stitch. When working the DS the next time, knit into both legs and treat as one stitch.

Shawl

CO 4 sts.

Row 1: (RS) [K1, yo] 3 times, k1—7 sts.

Row 2: (WS) [P1, p1 tbl] 3 times, p1.

Row 3: K2, [yo, k1] 3 times, yo, k2—11 sts.

Row 4: Sl 2 wyb, [p1 tbl, p1] to last 3 sts, p1 tbl, sl 2 wyb.

Row 5: Knit.

Row 6: Sl 2 wyb, purl to last 2 sts, sl 2 wyb.

Row 9: K2, [yo, k1] to last 2 sts, yo, k2—19 sts.

Row 10: Rep Row 4.

Rows 11–16: Rep Rows 5 and 6 three times.

Row 17: K3, [yo, k1] to last 3 sts, yo, k3—33 sts.

Row 18: Sl 2 wyb, [p1, p1 tbl] to last 3 sts, p1, sl 2 wyb.

Rows 19–32: Rep Rows 5 and 6 seven times.

Row 33: Rep Row 9—63 sts.

Row 34: Rep Row 4.

LACE SECTION 1

Row 1: (RS) K2, working Row 1 of Flame Chart 1, work first 4 sts at right edge of chart, rep next 7 sts 7 times, work rem 6 sts at left edge of chart, then k2.

Row 2 and all WS rows: Sl 2 wyb, purl to last 2 sts, sl 2 wyb.

Work Rows 3–24 of Flame Chart 1 as established, ending with a WS row.

Next (inc) row: (RS) [K2, yo] 3 times, [k1, yo] to last 8 sts, k2, [yo, k2] 3 times—118 sts.

Next row: (WS) Sl 2 wyb, [p1 tbl, p2] 3 times, [p1 tbl, p1] to last 6 sts, [p1 tbl, p2] twice, p1 tbl, sl 2 wyb.

LACE SECTION 2

Row 1: (RS) K2, working Row 1 of Flame Chart 2, work first 5 sts at right edge of chart, rep next 10 sts 10 times, work rem 9 sts at left edge of chart, then k2.

Row 2 and all WS rows: Sl 2 wyb, purl to last 2 sts, sl 2 wyb.

Work Rows 3–36 of Flame Chart 2 as established, ending with a WS row.

Next (inc) row: (RS) [K2, yo] twice, [k1, yo] to last 6 sts, [k2, yo] twice, k2—230 sts.

Next row: (WS) Sl 2 wyb, [p1 tbl, p2] twice, [p1 tbl, p1] to last 4 sts, p1 tbl, p2, p1 tbl, sl 2 wyb.

FLAME CHART 1

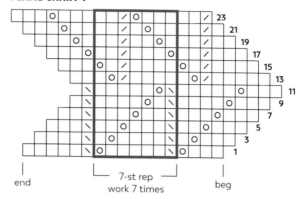

FLAME CHART 2

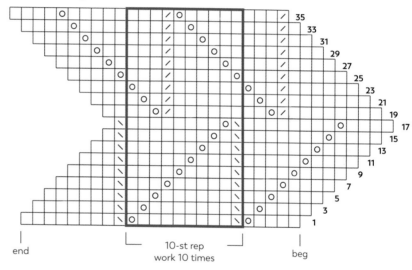

knit

○ yo

╱ k2tog

╲ ssk

▢ pattern repeat

FLAME CHART 3

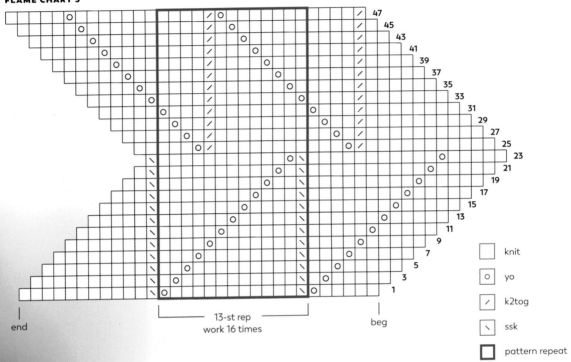

end

13-st rep
work 16 times

beg

	knit
○	yo
╱	k2tog
╲	ssk
▢	pattern repeat

FLAME CHART 4

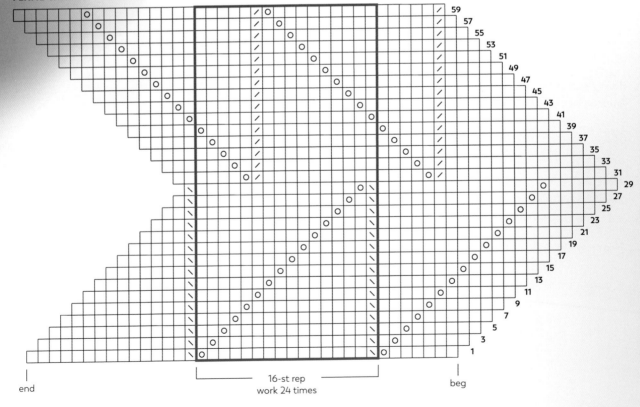

end

16-st rep
work 24 times

beg

LACE SECTION 3

Row 1: (RS) K2, working Row 1 of Flame Chart 3, work first 6 sts at right edge of chart, rep next 13 sts 16 times, work rem 12 sts at left edge of chart, then k2.

Row 2 and all WS rows: Sl 2 wyb, purl to last 2 sts, sl 2 wyb.

Work Rows 3–48 of Chart 3 as established, ending with a WS row.

Next (inc) row: (RS) K2, *[k1, yo] 3 times, k2, yo; rep from * to last 3 sts, k3—410 sts.

Next row: (WS) Sl 2 wyb, p1, *p1 tbl, p2, [p1 tbl, p1] 3 times; rep from * to last 2 sts, sl 2 wyb.

LACE SECTION 4

Row 1: (RS) K2, working Row 1 of Flame Chart 4, work first 7 sts at right edge of chart, rep next 16 sts 24 times, work rem 15 sts at left edge of chart, then k2.

Row 2 and all WS rows: Sl 2 wyb, purl to last 2 sts, sl 2 wyb.

Work Rows 3–60 of Flame Chart 4 as established, then rep Rows 1–30 once more, ending with a WS row.

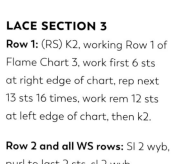

EDGING

Row 1: (RS) Knit.

Row 2: (WS) Sl 2 wyb, purl to last 2 sts, sl 2 wyb.

Rep Rows 1 and 2 once more.

The remainder of the edging will be worked in sections of 16 sts each, shaped with decreases and short-rows into flames.

> **NOTE** *The first stitch in Short-row 1 is only worked in the first repeat; in all following repeats the loop remaining on the right needle tip from the bind-off of the previous section becomes the first stitch of the next section.*

Short-row 1: (RS) Sl 1, ssk, k13, turn—15 sts rem.

Short-row 2: (WS) DS (see Stitch Guide), k14, turn.

Short-row 3: K1, ssk, k10, turn—14 sts rem.

Short-row 4: DS, k11, turn.

Short-row 5: K1, ssk, k7, turn—13 sts rem.

Short-row 6: DS, k8, turn.

Short-row 7: K1, ssk, k4, turn—12 sts rem.

Short-row 8: DS, k5, turn.

Short-row 9: K1, ssk, k1, turn—11 sts rem.

Short-row 10: DS, k2, turn.

BO row: (RS) Treating each DS as a single st, k1, [k1, return both sts to left needle tip and k2tog tbl] 11 times—1 st rem on right needle tip. Do not fasten off rem st.

Rep Short-rows 1–10 twenty-four more times—10 sts rem.

Final Edging Section

Short-row 1: (RS) Sl 1, ssk, k7, turn—9 sts rem.

Short-row 2: (WS) DS, k8, turn.

Short-row 3: K8, turn.

Short-row 4: DS, k7, turn.

Short-row 5: K1, ssk, k4, turn—8 sts rem.

Short-row 6: DS, k5, turn.

Short-row 7: K5, turn.

Short-row 8: DS, k4, turn.

Short-row 9: K1, ssk, k1, turn—7 sts rem.

Short-row 10: DS, k2, turn.

BO rem sts as described above. Fasten off last st.

Finishing

Weave in ends. Soak and block to measurements.

COLORWORK ROSES *socks*

Stranded knitting is a wonderful way to combine gradient and solid yarns. In these Scandinavian-inspired socks, a simple repeating pattern of roses and stripes is worked in creamy white, and a rose-colored gradient yarn fills in the background. The subtle changes in color give the graphic pattern a delicate feel. • **Aud Bergo**

FINISHED SIZES

7¾ (8¾)" (19.5 [22] cm) foot circumference, 10 (10½)" (25.5 [26.5] cm) foot length, and 9 (9¼)" (23 [23.5] cm) leg length from cuff to bottom of heel.

YARN

Fingering weight (#1 Super Fine).

Shown here: Jojoland Ballad (100% wool; 220 yd [200 m]/1¾ oz [50 g]): #BL002 Creamy White (MC), 2 balls.

Jojoland Melody Superwash (100% wool; 220 yd [200 m]/1¾ oz [50 g]): #MS102 Wax-flower (CC), 1 ball.

NEEDLES

Size U.S. 1½ (2.5 mm): two 16" or 24" (40 or 60 cm) circular (cir).

Size U.S. 1 (2.25 mm): two 16" cir.

Adjust needle size if necessary to obtain correct gauge.

NOTIONS

Tapestry needle.

GAUGE

36 sts and 36 rnds = 4" (10 cm) in colorwork patt with larger needles.

NOTES

• The pattern is written for using two short circular needles. The pattern can easily be used for one longer circular needle for the Magic Loop technique (see Glossary) or 5 double-pointed needles. The right and left sock are identical, and each round starts with Needle 1. Needle 1 is for the back of the leg, heel, gusset, and sole, and Needle 2 is for the front of the leg and instep.

• The stranded colorwork pattern is presented in chart form only. All charts are worked from right to left and from the bottom up, with the color for each stitch as shown. The chart for foot length will work well for a foot length up to about 10" (25.5 cm). For a shorter foot, end before the chart is finished. For a longer foot, either continue with additional rounds in MC only or add rounds from each section of the repeating pattern.

• Stranded colorwork can pull in and become inelastic without enough slack in the floats. Make the floats slack and, if in doubt, make them looser than you think they should be. For floats longer than 4 stitches, twist the yarn not in use around the working yarn to avoid long floats.

• For the best result, hold each of the two colors in the same position on your fingers throughout the whole work.

• The heel and toe are worked with the main color only. For this, use a smaller needle.

Before you begin, cut two strands of main color about 20" (51 cm) long to use for picking up stitches along the heel flap, using one strand for each sock.

Cuff

With MC and one larger cir needle, CO 70 (78) sts. Do not join.

Knit 1 row and distribute sts over 2 larger cir needles, with 35 (39) sts on each needle. Turn work and join for working in rnds, being careful not to twist sts.

Working from appropriate chart, work Rnd 1, until cuff measures 1½" (3.8 cm).

Leg

Work Rnds 2–46 of appropriate Leg chart. Piece should measure 6½" (16.5 cm). Both yarns are at the end of Needle 2.

With MC, k35 (39) sts from Needle 1, leaving rem 35 (39) sts on Needle 2 unworked.

Foot

HEEL FLAP

Beg working back and forth over sts on Needle 1 with MC only.

Change to smaller cir needle.

Row 1: (WS) Sl 1 wyf, p16 (18), M1P, purl to end of row—36 (40) sts.

Row 2: (RS) *Sl 1 wyb, k1; rep from * to end of row.

Row 3: (WS) Sl 1 wyf, purl to end of row.

Rep Rows 2 and 3 until flap measures 2½–2¾" (6.5–7 cm), ending with a RS row.

SIZE 7¾" (19.5 CM) LEG CHART

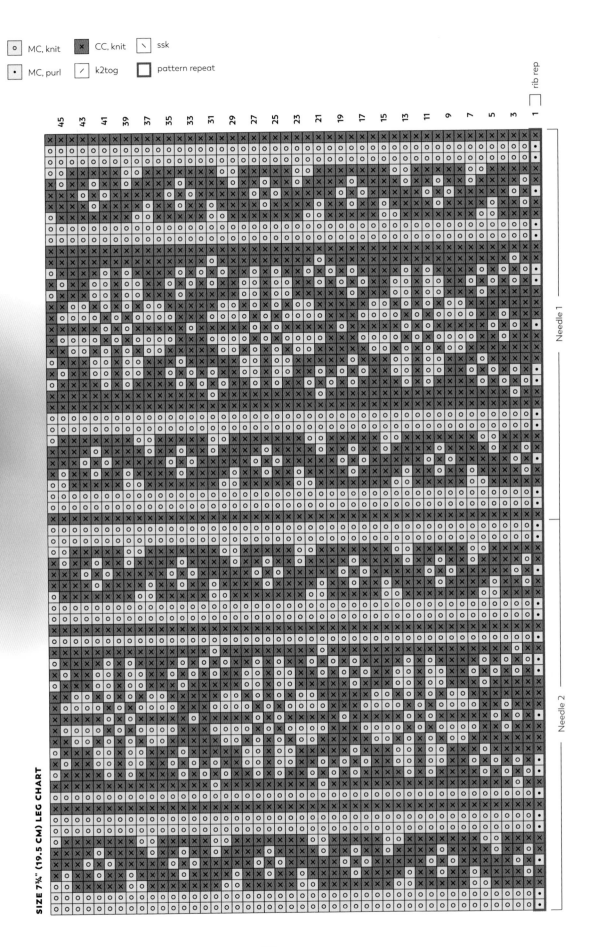

Needle 2

Needle 1

rib rep

TURN HEEL

Row 1: (WS) Sl 1 wyf, p20
(22), p2tog, p1, turn.

Row 2: (RS) Sl 1 wyb, k7, ssk, k1, turn.

Row 3: (WS) Sl 1 wyf, purl to 1 st
before gap, p2tog, p1, turn—1 st dec'd.

Row 4: (RS) Sl 1 wyb, knit to 1 st
before gap, ssk, k1, turn—1 st dec'd.

Rep Rows 3 and 4 until all sts have
been worked—22 (24) sts rem.

GUSSET SET-UP

With MC and RS facing, pick up and
knit 17 sts along left edge of heel flap.
With 20" (51 cm) length of MC, pick
up and knit 17 sts along right edge of
heel flap—56 (58) sts on Needle 1.

Next row: (WS) Sl 1 wyf, purl to
end of row and dec 1 st at center
of heel—57 (59) sts rem.

GUSSET AND FOOT CHART
(SOLE AND INSTEP)

Change Needle 1 to larger
cir needle. Join for working in
rnds again—92 (98) sts.

Work Rnds 1–58 of appropriate
Gusset and Foot chart—70 (78) sts
rem when gusset shaping is complete.
Foot should measure about 8 (8¼)"
(20.5 [21] cm) from back of heel.
See pattern notes if foot length
needs to be adjusted. The toe will
measure about 2 (2¼)" (5 [5.5] cm).

Needle 2

Needle 1

1 3 5 7 9 11 13 15 17 19 21 23 25 27 29 31 33 35 37 39 41 43 45 47 49 51 53 55 57

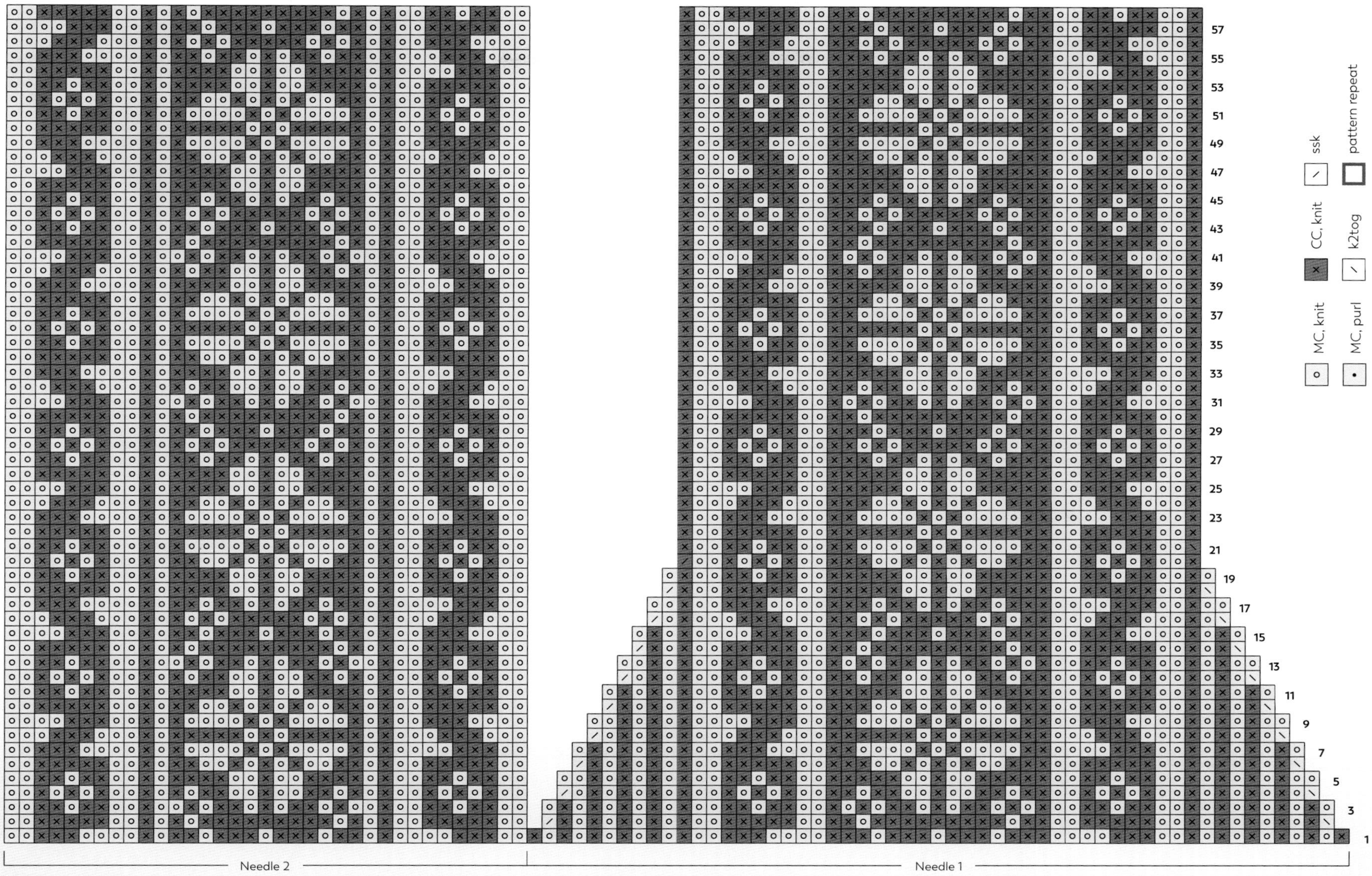

| | MC, knit | | CC, knit | | ssk |
| | MC, purl | | k2tog | | pattern repeat |

Toe

Cut CC. Change to smaller cir needles.

Rnds 1 and 2: Knit.

Rnd 3: (dec) *K1, ssk, knit to last 3 sts on needle, k2tog, k1; rep from * once more—4 sts dec'd.

Rep dec rnd every other rnd 4 more times, then every rnd 9 (11) times—14 sts rem.

Cut yarn, leaving an 8" (20.5 cm) tail, thread tail through rem sts, pulling tight to close hole, fasten off on WS.

Finishing

Weave in ends. Block to measurements.

Needle 2

Needle 1

1 3 5 7 9 11 13 15 17 19 21 23 25 27 29 31 33 35 37 39 41 43 45 47 49 51 53 55 57

| | MC, knit | | CC, knit | | ssk |
| | MC, purl | | k2tog | | pattern repeat |

OCEAN WAVES *cowl*

This show-stopping cowl is knit in the round from the center out, ending in a beautiful feather-and-fan border on each end. The brilliant blues and greens that evoke clear, sparkling ocean waters fade out symmetrically. The cowl is wide enough to be worn draped over your shoulders or looped twice around your neck for extra warmth. • **Toby Roxane Barna**

FINISHED SIZE
About 52½" (133.5 cm) circumference at center and 13¾" (35 cm) long.

YARN
Fingering weight (#1 Super Fine).

Shown here: A Hundred Ravens Iachos Mini Skein Set (100% merino wool; 400 yd [366 m]/3½ oz [100 g]): Mermaid's Tail, 2 sets. Label the 7 mini skeins A–G, from turquoise blue (A) to green (G).

NEEDLES
Size U.S. 6 (4 mm): 24" (60 cm) circular (cir).

Adjust needle size if necessary to obtain the correct gauge.

NOTIONS
Size G or H (4 or 5 mm) crochet hook for provisional cast-on; about 9 yd (8 m) of waste yarn for cast-on; markers (m); tapestry needle.

GAUGE
22 sts and 49 rows = 4" (10 cm) in Garter st.

NOTE
• This cowl is knit in the round from the center out. First, stitches are provisionally cast on and worked toward one edge using one complete gradient set, then stitches are picked up from the provisional cast-on, and the other half of the cowl is knit toward the opposite edge using the second gradient set.

Feather and Fan Worked in the Rnd (multiple of 17 sts)

Rnd 1: *[K2tog] 3 times, [yo, k1] 5 times, yo, [ssk] 3 times; rep from * to end of rnd.

Rnds 2 and 4: Knit.

Rnd 3: Purl.

Rep Rnds 1–4 for patt.

Cowl

FIRST HALF

Using crochet hook and waste yarn, CO 289 sts with A using the provisional method (see Glossary). Place marker (pm) and join for working in rnds, being careful not to twist sts.

Work in garter st (purl 1 rnd, knit 1 rnd), *changing to next gradient shade as each color is used up until last 3 colors of first gradient set rem. Change to third-to-last color and finish rnd. Work 2 or 3 more rnds, ending with a purl rnd.

Work Rnds 1–4 of feather and fan (see Stitch Guide or chart), changing to next gradient shade as needed. When 8 rnds of last color have been worked, BO all sts as foll:

[K2tog tbl (see Glossary), place st on RH needle back onto LH needle] until 1 st rem. Fasten off rem st.*

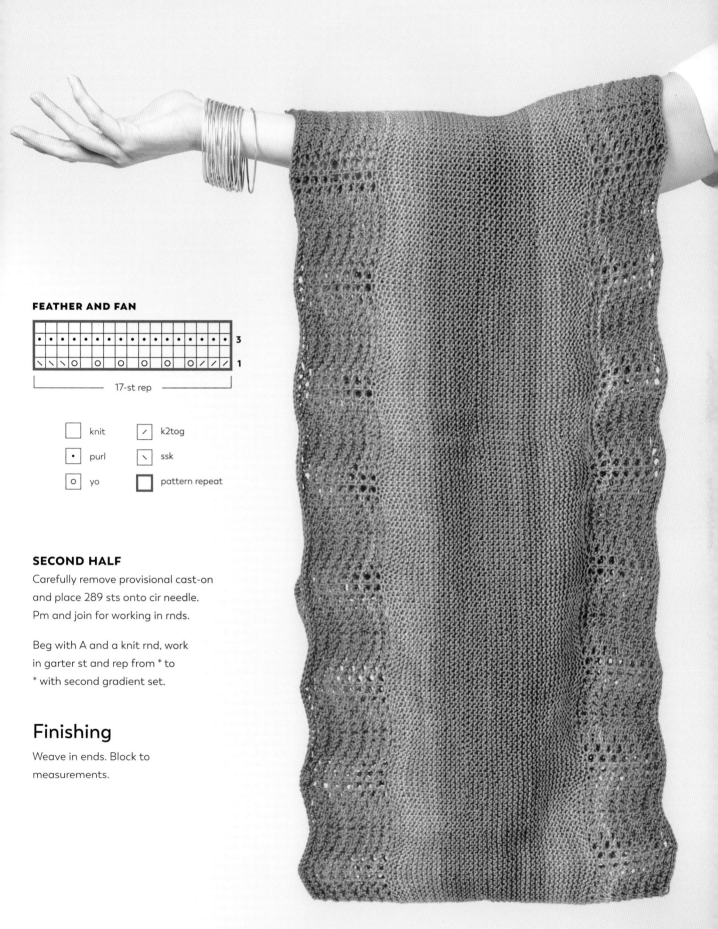

FEATHER AND FAN

17-st rep

knit

• purl

o yo

/ k2tog

\ ssk

pattern repeat

SECOND HALF

Carefully remove provisional cast-on
and place 289 sts onto cir needle.
Pm and join for working in rnds.

Beg with A and a knit rnd, work
in garter st and rep from * to
* with second gradient set.

Finishing

Weave in ends. Block to
measurements.

DENIM STRIPES
cardigan

As classic and comfortable as a well-worn pair of jeans, you'll want to wear this boyfriend cardigan every day. The color patterns gently shift from dark to light in a pleasing gradient as the sweater is knit from the top down. Eight shades of blue alternate with a subtly contrasting gray yarn in a skinny stripes pattern. • **Kathryn Folkerth**

FINISHED SIZES

About 36¼ (39¾, 44¼, 48½, 52¾)" (92 [101, 112.5, 123, 134] cm) bust circumference and 26½ (26½, 28, 28, 28)" (67.5 [67.5, 71, 71, 71] cm) long.

Cardigan shown measures 39¾" (101 cm).

YARN

Fingering Weight (#1 Super Fine).

Shown here:
Jamieson's Shetland Spindrift (100% Shetland wool; 115 yd [105 m]/.88 oz [25 g]): #122 Granite (MC), 6 (7, 8, 9, 10) balls; #726 Prussian Blue (CC1), 1 ball; #684 Cobalt (CC2), 1 ball; #700 Royal (CC3), 1 ball; #168 Clyde Blue (CC4), 1 ball; #685 Delph (CC5), 1 ball; #665 Bluebell (CC6), 1 ball; #136 Teviot (CC7), 1 ball; #134 Blue Danube (CC8), 1 ball.

NEEDLES

Size U.S. 4 (3.5 mm): 32" (80 cm) circular (cir), and cir or double-pointed (dpn) for preferred method of working small circumferences in the round.

Size U.S. 3 (3.25 mm): 40" (100 cm) cir and cir or dpn for preferred method of working small circumferences in the round.

Adjust needle size if necessary to obtain the correct gauge.

NOTIONS

Markers (m); stitch holders or waste yarn; tapestry needle; seven ¾" (19 mm) buttons.

GAUGE

26 sts and 36 rows/ rnds = 4" (10 cm) in St st with larger needles.

NOTES

• Increase only on MC rows.

• For RS Raglan inc rows, work M1R before markers and M1L after markers.

For WS Raglan inc rows, work a M1P-R before markers and M1P-L after markers.

• You will be working two RS rows followed by two WS rows as follows: Work the first RS row with MC, slide the stitches back to the opposite end of the needle without turning, work the second RS row with CC, then turn. Work the first WS row with MC, slide the stitches back to the opposite end of the needle without turning, work the second WS row with CC, then turn.

STITCH GUIDE

K2, P2 Rib (multiple of 4 sts + 2)
Row 1: (RS) *K2, p2; rep from * to last 2 sts, k2.

Row 2: (WS) P2, *k2, p2; rep from * to end of row.

Rep Rows 1 and 2 for patt.

Stripe Pattern
Rows 1 and 2: (RS) Working in St st, work Row 1 with MC, then work Row 2 with CC1.

Rows 3 and 4: (WS) Working in St st, work Row 3 with MC, then work Row 4 with CC1.

Rows 5–22 (22, 24, 24, 24): Rep last 4 rows 4 (4, 5, 5, 5) more times, then work Rows 1 and 2 one (1, 0, 0, 0) more time(s).

Next row: Work with MC.

Next row: Join CC2 and work 1 row.

Next row: Work with MC.

Next row: Work with CC1.

Rep last 4 rows once more. Cut CC1.

***Next row:** Work with MC.

Next row: Work with CC2.

Rep last 2 rows 10 (10, 11, 11, 11) more times.

Next row: Work with MC.

Next row: Join CC3 and work 1 row.

Next row: Work with MC.

Next row: Work with CC2.

Rep last 4 rows once more. Cut CC2.

Rep from * 5 more times, then work 10 rows with MC and CC8.

Yoke

With longer, larger cir needle and MC, CO 74 (76, 80, 84, 92) sts. Do not join.

Row 1: (RS) K2 for left front, place marker (pm), k12 (12, 12, 12, 14) for sleeve, pm, k46 (48, 52, 56, 60) for back, pm, k12 (12, 12, 12, 14) for sleeve, pm, k2 for right front. Slide sts back to opposite end of needle.

Row 2: (RS) Join CC1 and knit, slipping m as you come to them. Turn work.

Cont in Stripe patt from Row 3.

Raglan inc row: (WS) *Purl to 1 st before m, M1P-R, p1, sl m, p1, M1P-L; repeat from * 3 more times, then purl to end of row—8 sts inc'd.

Work 1 WS row even with CC.

back & front

35½ (39, 43½, 47¾, 52)"
90 (99, 110.5, 121.5, 132) cm
with ¾" (2 cm) gap

16¾ (16¼, 17, 16¾, 15½)"
42.5 (41.5, 43, 42.5, 39.5) cm

13 (14½, 16½, 17½, 19½)"
33 (37, 42, 44.5, 49.5) cm

9¼ (9¾, 10½, 11, 11¾)"
23.5 (25, 26.5, 28, 30) cm

8¾ (9¼, 10, 10¼, 11½)"
22 (23.5, 25.5, 26, 29) cm

1"
2.5 cm

16¾ (16¼, 17, 16¾, 15½)"
42.5 (41.5, 43, 42.5, 39.5) cm

7 (7½, 8, 8½, 9¼)"
18 (19, 20.5, 21.5, 23.5 cm)

Raglan inc row: (RS) *Knit to 1 st before m, M1R, k1, sl m, k1, M1L; rep from * 3 more times, then knit to end of row—8 sts inc'd.

Work 1 RS row even with CC.

Working all raglan and neck shaping on MC rows, work CC rows even on RS and WS, cont in Stripe patt and shape raglan and neck as foll.

Sizes 36¼ (39¾, 44¼)" (92 [101, 112.5] cm only

Raglan and neck inc row: (WS) K1, M1P-L, *purl to 1 st before m, M1P-R, p1, sl m, p1, M1P-L; rep from * 3 more times, purl to last st, M1P-R, p1—10 sts inc'd.

Next MC row: (RS) Rep Raglan inc row—8 sts inc'd.

[Work Raglan and neck inc row on next MC row, then work Raglan inc row on next MC row] 6 (6, 8) times—216 (218, 258) sts, with 44 (44, 52) sts for each sleeve, 25 (25, 31) sts for each front, and 78 (80, 92) sts for back. Make sure to work increases M1L and M1R on RS rows, and M1P-L and M1P-R on WS rows (see Notes).

Rep Raglan and neck inc row every other MC row 8 (5, 3) times—296 (268, 288) sts, with 60 (54, 58) sts for each sleeve, 41 (35, 37) sts for each front, and 94 (90, 98) sts for back.

[Work Raglan and neck inc row on next MC row, then work Raglan inc row on next MC row] 3 (7, 9) times, then work Raglan inc row on next 1 (1, 0) MC row(s)—358 (402, 450) sts, with 74 (84, 94) sts for each sleeve, 57 (56, 64) sts for each front, and 108

(120, 134) sts for back. Piece should measure about 8¾ (9¼, 10)" (22 [23.5, 25.5] cm) from beg at back neck.

Sizes 48½ (52¾)"
(123 [134] cm) only
Next MC row: (WS) Rep Raglan inc row—8 sts inc'd.

Raglan and neck inc row: (RS) K1, M1L, knit to 1 st before m, M1R, k1, sl m, k1, M1L; rep from * 3 more times, then knit to last st, M1R—10 sts inc'd.

[Work Raglan inc row on next MC row, work Raglan and neck inc row on next MC row] 19 (22) times, work Raglan inc row on next MC row, then work Raglan and neck inc row every MC row 3 (2) times—498 (550) sts, with 104 (116) sts for each sleeve, 71 (78) sts for each front, and 148 (162) sts for back. Make sure to work increases M1L and M1R on RS rows, and M1P-L and M1P-R on WS rows (see Notes).

Piece should measure about 10¼ (11½)" (26 [29] cm) from beg at back neck.

All sizes
DIVIDE FOR BODY AND SLEEVES
Next row: *Work in established patt to m, remove m, place 74 (84, 94, 104, 116) sleeve sts onto holder or waste yarn, remove m, CO 10 (10, 15, 10, 10) sts using the backward-loop method (see Glossary); rep from * once more, then work to end of row—230 (254, 282, 310, 338) sts.

Body

Cont even until Stripe patt is complete. Piece should measure 24½ (24½, 26, 26, 26)" (62 [62, 66, 66, 66] cm) from beg at back neck. Cut CC8.

Change to longer, smaller cir needle.

Beg with a RS (RS, WS, WS, WS) row and work in k2, p2 rib (see Stitch Guide) for 1" (2.5 cm).

BO all sts loosely in patt.

Sleeves

Return held 74 (84, 94, 104, 116) sleeve sts to larger needles. With RS facing and next stripe color, beg at center of underarm, pick up and knit 5 (5, 7, 5, 5) sts along underarm CO, knit sleeve sts, then pick up and knit 5 (5, 7, 5, 5) sts along rem underarm CO edge—84 (94, 108, 114, 126) sts. Pm and join for working in rnds.

Work 1 rnd even.

Dec rnd: K1, k2tog, knit to last 3 sts, ssk, k1—2 sts dec'd.

Rep Dec rnd every 12 (10, 8, 8, 6) rnds 11 (7, 11, 6, 12) times, then every 0 (8, 6, 6, 4) rnds 0 (7, 8, 14, 12) times—60 (64, 68, 72, 76) sts rem.

Cont even until Stripe patt is complete. Sleeve should measure 15¾ (15¼, 16, 15¾, 14½)" (40 [38.5, 40.5, 40, 37] cm). Cut C8.

Change to smaller needles.

Next rnd: *K2, p2; rep from * around.

Rep last rnd until ribbing measures 1" (2.5 cm).

BO all sts loosely in rib.

Buttonband

With longer smaller cir needle and MC, pick up and knit 150 (151, 159, 159, 161) sts (about 3 sts for every 4 rows) along right front edge, 70 (72, 76, 80, 88) sts (1 st in every st) along top of sleeves and back neck, 150 (151, 159, 159, 161) sts along left front edge—370 (374, 394, 398, 410) sts. Do not join.

Beg with a WS row, work 3 rows in k2, p2 Rib. Pm for 7 buttons along right front, with top m at end of neck shaping, bottom m 4 sts from bottom edge, then evenly space rem m in between.

Buttonhole row: (RS) *Work to m in established ribbing, work a one-row buttonhole (see Glossary) over next 2 sts; rep from * 6 more times, then work to end of row.

Work 3 more rows of ribbing. BO all sts in patt.

Finishing

Join underarms using Kitchener st (see Glossary).

Weave in ends. Block to measurements.

Sew buttons to left front opposite buttonholes.

CABLED *hat*

This fun-to-knit topper celebrates color and texture as multidirectional cables meander across a gorgeous gradient of greens and yellows. A whimsical braided cord cinches the hat at the top. Attach a bead to each braid for an extra-special finish. • **Karen Bourquin**

FINISHED SIZE

18" (45.5 cm) brim circumference and 10½" (26.5 cm) tall.

YARN

Sock weight (#1 Super Fine).

Shown here: SweetGeorgia Yarns Tough Love Sock

"Party of Five" Mini-Skein Set (80% merino wool, 20% nylon; 525 yd [480 m]/5 oz [142 g]): Botanica, 1 pack; colors include 4th and Vine (A), Basil (B), Pistachio (C), Melon (D), and Sourpuss (E).

NEEDLES

Size U.S. 2 (2.75 mm): 24" (60 cm) circular (cir).

Size U.S. 3 (3.25 mm): 24" (60 cm) cir.

Adjust needle sizes if necessary to achieve the correct gauge.

NOTIONS

Cable needle (cn); markers (m); waste yarn; safety pin; 2 beads ½" (13 mm); tapestry needle.

GAUGE

22½ sts and 38 rnds = 4" (10 cm) in cable pattern with larger needle.

STITCH GUIDE

Cable Pattern (multiple of 12 sts)

Rnds 1 and 2: *K2, p2; rep from * to end of rnd.

Rnd 3: *2/2/2 RC, p2, k2, p2; rep from * to end of rnd.

Rnds 4–8: Rep Rnd 1.

Rnd 9: *K2, p2, 2/2/2 LC, p2; rep from * to end of rnd.

Rnds 10–12: Rep Rnd 1.

Rep Rnds 1–12 for patt.

2/2/2 RC (2 over 2 over 2 right cross): Sl 4 sts onto cn and hold at back of work, k2, sl 2 purl sts from cn back to LH needle, p2, then k2 from cn.

2/2/2 LC (2 over 2 over 2 left cross): Sl 4 sts onto cn and hold at front of work, k2, sl 2 purl sts from cn back to LH needle, p2, then k2 from cn.

3-strand Braid Divide strands into 3 groups and spread slightly apart. *Pick up strand on right side and place between other 2 strands. Pick up strand on left side and place between the 2 strands. Rep from * for desired length.

Hat

With smaller cir needle and waste yarn, CO 132 sts with A using the provisional method (see Glossary). Place marker (pm) and join for working in rnds, being careful to not twist sts.

Work 1½" (3.8 cm) of St st (knit every rnd).

Next rnd: Purl.

Change to larger cir needle.

Next rnd: *K2, p2; rep from * to end of rnd.

Rep last rnd until ribbing measures 1½" (3.8 cm).

Carefully remove provisional CO and place resulting 132 sts onto smaller cir needle. Fold piece at purl rnd with WS tog (RS facing) and larger cir needle in front.

CABLE CHART

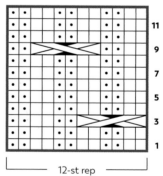

12-st rep

| | knit |
| · | purl |
| 2/2/2 LC (see Stitch Guide) |
| 2/2/2 RC (see Stitch Guide) |
| | pattern repeat |

Joining rnd: *[Knit tog 1 st each from front and back needles] twice, [purl tog 1 st each from front and back needles] twice; rep from * to end of rnd—132 sts.

Beg with Rnd 2 of cable patt (see Stitch Guide or chart), work 16 rnds. Cut A.

Join B, and work in established patt for 19 rnds. Cut B.

Join C, and work in established patt for 19 rnds. Cut C.

Join D, and work in established patt for 19 rnds. Cut D.

Join E, and work in established patt for 3 rnds, ending with Rnd 5 of patt. Piece should measure about 9½" (24 cm) from fold.

Change to smaller cir needle.

Next 2 rnds: *K2, p2; rep from * to end of rnd.

Eyelet rnd: K2, p2, [yo] twice, k2tog, cont in established rib to last 6 sts, [yo] twice, k2tog, k2, p2.

Next rnd: K2, p2, k1 and drop extra yo, cont in established rib to last 6 sts, p1 and drop extra yo, p1, k2, p2.

Work in established rib for 6 more rnds.

Next rnd: Purl.

Work in St st for 1½" (3.8 cm).

BO all sts loosely. Cut yarn, leaving a 24" (61 cm) tail.

NOTE *Use larger cir needle if desired to ensure a looser BO.*

Finishing
Fold top edge along purl rnd to inside. Sew BO edge to WS.

Weave in ends. Block to measurements, taking care not to flatten cables.

BRAIDED CORD
Cut 5 strands of yarn (1 of each color), each 30" (76 cm) long.

Holding all strands tog, tie a knot in one end about 3" (7.5 cm) from ends. Divide strands into 3 sections, with 2 strands in each of first and third sections, and 1 strand in second section. Work 3-strand Braid (see Stitch Guide) until 3" (7.5 cm) remain at ends of strands. Knot ends.

Attach a safety pin in knot at one end of cord and thread through first eyelet and through casing at top of hat. Exit cord through second eyelet. Remove safety pin and slip a bead to each end of cord. Tie another knot over the original knot to secure beads in place. Pull up cord tight to gather top of hat and tie in a bow.

CHEVRON *cowl*

Snuggle up with this squishy neck warmer. The simple knit-and-purl chevron pattern lets the beauty of the gradient yarn shine. Alternating two skeins of the same yarn maintains the gradient while extending the length of the cowl. • **Tian Connaughton**

FINISHED SIZE
About 30½" (77.5 cm) circumference and 13" (33 cm) high.

YARN
Sportweight (#2 Fine).

Shown here: Freia Fibers Ombré Sport Gradient (100% wool; 217 yd [198 m]/2½ oz [75 g]): Mist, 2 balls.

NEEDLES
Size U.S. 6 (4 mm): 24" or 32" (60 or 80 cm) circular (cir).

Adjust needle size if necessary to achieve the correct gauge.

NOTIONS
Marker (m); tapestry needle.

GAUGE
23½ sts and 41 rnds = 4" (10 cm) in stitch patt.

NOTE
• The cowl is worked in the round from the bottom up. The pattern uses two skeins. In order to maintain the color block, alternate skeins every round, making sure to start at the same color in each skein.

K2, P2 Rib (multiple of 4 sts)

All rnds: *K2, p2; rep from * around.

Chevron Pattern (multiple of 18 sts)

Rnd 1: *K1, p1, k2, p2, k2, p1; rep from * around.

Rnd 2: *K3, p2, k2, p2, k1, [p2, k2] twice; rep from * around.

Rnd 3: *[K2, p2] twice, k3, p2, k2, p2, k1; rep from * around.

Rnd 4: *K1, p2, k2, p2, k5, p2, k2, p2; rep from * around.

Rep rnds 1–4 for patt.

CHEVRON CHART

18-st rep

☐ knit

▪ purl

☐ pattern repeat

Cowl

CO 180 sts. Place marker (pm), and join for working in rnds, taking care not to twist sts.

Work in k2, p2 rib (see Stitch Guide) for 1½" (3.8 cm).

Work Rnds 1–4 of chevron patt (see Stitch Guide or chart) until piece measures 11½" (29 cm) from CO edge.

Work in k2, p2 rib for 1½" (3.8 cm).

BO all sts loosely in patt.

Finishing

Weave in ends. Block to measurements.

SHAPE-SHIFTER *scarf*

This scarf highlights the changes in a color-shifting yarn with a simple intarsia pattern worked in garter stitch. It has a bold graphic look created by using the same color yarn from opposite ends of the ball. Try working the scarf with one side in a color-shifting yarn and the other in a complementary solid color for a completely different look. • **Natalie Servant**

FINISHED SIZE

About 10" (25.5 cm) wide and 60" (152.5 cm) long.

YARN

Worsted weight (#4 Medium).

Shown here: The Blue Brick Tobermory Worsted (100% merino wool; 200 yd [183 m]/4¾ oz [135 g]): Berry Vanilla, 3 skeins. (See Notes for how to designate yarn as C1 and C2.)

NEEDLES

Size U.S. 7 (4.5 mm).

Adjust needle size if necessary to achieve the correct gauge.

NOTIONS

Marker (m); tapestry needle.

GAUGE

17 sts and 36½ rows = 4" (10 cm) in garter st (knit every row).

NOTES

• The pattern is worked with two balls of yarn using the intarsia technique. C1 is the first ball, C2 is the second ball, started from the opposite end of the color shift. The two balls are both used on each row, and the dividing point is marked with a stitch marker. The change from one color to another is always done on the wrong side of the scarf by bringing the new color up from under the old color.

• The first stitch of each row is slipped purlwise with the yarn in front, creating a tidy chain along the sides.

• When beginning the third skein, work C1 from one end of the skein and C2 from the other end of the skein.

Scarf

With C1, CO 28 sts, place marker (pm), with C2, CO 17 sts—45 sts.

Next row: (WS) With C2, knit to marker, sl m, bring C1 up from under C2 and knit to end of row.

Next 4 rows: Sl 1 wyf, knit to m, sl m, bring new color up from under old color and knit to end of row.

Next row: (RS) Working Row 1 of Wave chart, sl 1 wyf, knit to 3 sts before m, k2tog, k1, sl m, bring new color up from under old color, k1, k1f&b, knit to end of row.

Next row: (WS) Working Row 2 of Wave chart, sl 1 wyf, knit to marker, sl m, bring new color up from under old color, knit to end of row.

Work Rows 3–68 of Wave chart, then rep Rows 1–68 seven more times. Piece should measure about 60" (152.5 cm) from beg.

BO all sts using C1 to m, remove m, bring C2 up from under C1, then BO to end of row.

Finishing

Weave in ends. Wet-block to measurements.

WAVE CHART

45 sts

	C1
	C2
	k on RS, p on WS
•	p on RS, k on WS
/	k2tog
\	ssk
V	sl 1 wyf on WS
ⱴ	sl 1 wyf on RS
Y	k1f&b (see Glossary)
	pattern repeat

GRAY-SCALE *cardigan*

A wide collar knit in a subtle gradient of beautiful grays takes center stage in this elegantly striking cardigan. The reversible textured stitch pattern makes the collar pop against the stockinette-stitch body. Waist shaping and set-in sleeves lend a tailored vibe. • **Emma Welford**

FINISHED SIZES

33 (36¾, 40¾, 44½, 48½, 52½)" (84 [93.5, 103.5, 113, 123, 133.5] cm) bust circumference with 2 (2, 2½, 2¼, 2¼, 2¼)" (5 [5, 6.5, 5.5, 5.5, 5.5] cm) gap at front and 25¼ (25½, 26, 26¼, 26¾, 27¼)" 64 (65, 66, 66.5, 68, 70] cm) long.

Cardigan shown measures 36¾" (93.5 cm).

YARN

Worsted weight (#4 Medium).

Shown here: Cascade Yarns 220 Superwash (100% superwash wool; 220 yd [201 m]/3½ oz [100 g]): #1913 Jet (MC), 5 (6, 6, 7, 7, 8) skeins.

Cascade Yarns 220 Superwash Wave (100% superwash wool; 220 yd [201 m]/3½ oz [100 g]): #110 Graphite (CC), 2 skeins.

NEEDLES

Size U.S. 5 (3.75 mm): 32" (80 cm) circular (cir).

Size U.S. 6 (4 mm): 32" (80 cm) cir and set of double-pointed (dpn).

Adjust needle size if necessary to achieve the correct gauge.

NOTIONS

Markers (m); waste yarn; stitch holders; 2 toggles; matching sewing thread and needle; tapestry needle.

GAUGE

20½ sts and 28 rows = 4" (10 cm) in St st with larger needles.

25 sts and 28 rows = 4" (10 cm) in rosette stitch with larger needles.

NOTES

• The Gray-scale Cardigan is worked from the bottom up in one piece. The body and sleeves are worked separately to the underarm, then joined together and worked as one to shape the upper body, sleeve caps, and shoulders. The collar is worked at the same time as the body for minimal seaming. Make sure to twist your MC and CC strands around each other when changing colors to avoid a hole.

• You'll be working from two balls of yarn for the collar, one on each side of the front. If you want the collar fronts to match exactly, start at the same point in the color gradient or shift for each CO edge of the collar.

• Placing the toggles closer or farther away from the front edges will change the bust circumference.

Body

With larger needles and waste yarn, use the provisional method (see Glossary) to CO 30 sts with CC, place marker (pm), join MC and CO 140 (160, 180, 200, 220, 240) sts, pm, then CO join another ball of CC and 30 sts—200 (220, 240, 260, 280, 300) sts. Do not join.

Row 1: (WS) With CC, knit to m, sl m, bring MC up from under CC to twist yarns, knit to m, sl m, bring CC up from under MC to twist yarns, then knit to end of row.

Row 2: (RS) With CC, k2, work Row 1 of rosette st (see Stitch guide) to m, sl m, bring MC up from under CC to twist yarns, knit to m, sl m, bring CC up from under MC to twist yarns, work Row 1 of rosette st to last 2 sts, k2.

Row 3: With CC, k2, work in patt to m, sl m, bring MC up from under CC to twist yarns, purl to m, sl m, bring CC up from under CC to twist yarns, work in patt to last 2 sts, k2.

Cont in established patt, keeping first 2 sts and last 2 sts in Garter st (knit every row), working rosette st bands with CC, and body with MC in St st (knit RS rows, purl WS rows), until piece measures 6" (15 cm) from beg, ending with a WS row.

SHAPE BODY

Set-up row: (RS) Work 47 (50, 53, 55, 58, 60) sts in established patt, pm for dart, k36 (40, 44, 50, 54, 60), pm for dart, k34 (40, 46, 50, 56, 60), pm for dart, k36 (40, 44, 50, 54, 60), pm for dart, then work to end of row.

Work 1 WS row even.

Dec row: (RS) Work in established patt to dart m, sl m, k2tog, knit to 2 sts before next dart m, ssk, sl m, knit to next dart m, sl m, k2tog, knit to 2 sts before next dart m, ssk, sl m, then work to end of row—4 sts dec'd.

Rep Dec row every 10 rows 4 more times—180 (200, 220, 240, 260, 280) sts rem. Remove dart m.

Work even until piece measures 17" (43 cm) from beg, ending with a WS row. Set body aside.

Sleeves

With dpn and MC, CO 35 (37, 39, 41, 43, 45) sts. Pm and join for working in rnds, being careful not to twist sts.

Rnd 1: Knit.

Rnd 2: Purl.

Rep Rnds 1 and 2 until piece measures 4" (10 cm) from beg, ending with a purl rnd.

Work 2 rnds in St st (knit every rnd).

Inc rnd: K2, M1L, knit to last 2 sts, M1R, k2—2 sts inc'd.

Rep Inc rnd every 6 (6, 5, 5, 4, 4) rnds 13 (14, 16, 17, 20, 23) more times—63 (67, 73, 77, 85, 93) sts.

Cont even until piece measures 17 (17½, 17½, 18, 18, 18)" (43 [44.5, 44.5, 45.5, 45.5, 45.5 cm) from beg, ending last rnd 5 (5, 5, 6, 6, 6) sts before end of rnd.

Place next 10 (10, 10, 12, 12, 12) sts on holder—53 (57, 63, 65, 73, 81) sts rem.

Yoke

Joining row: (RS) Work 40 (45, 50, 54, 59, 64) sts in established patt for left front, pm for armhole, place next 10 (10, 10, 12, 12, 12) sts onto holder for armhole, knit 53 (57, 63, 65, 73, 81) sleeve sts, pm for armhole, k80 (90, 100, 108, 118, 128) sts for back, pm for armhole, place next 10 (10, 10, 12, 12, 12) sts onto holder for armhole, knit 53 (57, 63, 65, 73, 81) sleeve sts, pm for armhole, then work to end of row—266 (294, 326, 346, 382, 418) sts.

Work 5 (3, 5, 5, 5, 5) rows even.

Sizes 36¾ (44½, 48½, 52½)" (93.5 [113, 123, 133.5] cm) only

Next (dec) row: (RS) *Work in established patt to 2 sts before armhole m, ssk, sl m, knit to m, sl m, k2tog; rep from * once more, then work to end of row—290 (342, 378, 414) sts rem, with 57 (65, 73, 81) sts for each sleeve, 44 (53, 58, 63) sts for each front, and 88 (106, 116, 126) sts for back.

Work 1 row even.

All sizes

Dec row 1: (RS) *Work to 2 sts before armhole m, ssk, sl m, k2tog; rep from * 3 more times, then work to end of row—8 sts dec'd.

Dec row 2: (WS) *Work to 2 sts before armhole m, p2tog, sl m, ssp; rep from * 3 more times, then work to end of row—8 sts dec'd.

Rep last 2 rows 1 (2, 4, 5, 7, 9) time(s) more—234 (242, 246, 246, 250, 254) sts rem, with 45 (45, 43, 41, 41, 41) sts for each sleeve, 36 (38, 40, 41, 42, 43) sts for each front, and 72 (76, 80, 82, 84, 86) back sts.

back & front

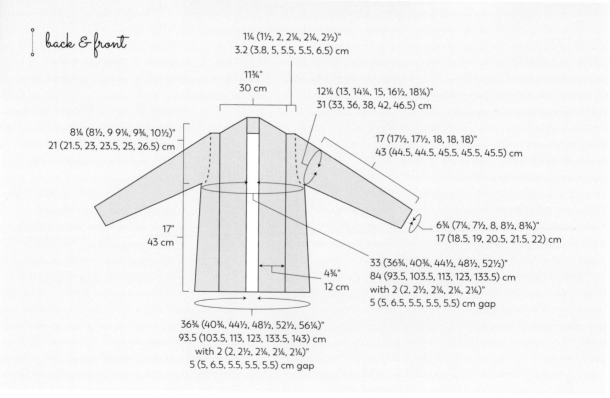

1¼ (1½, 2, 2¼, 2¼, 2½)"
3.2 (3.8, 5, 5.5, 5.5, 6.5) cm

11¾"
30 cm

12¼ (13, 14¼, 15, 16½, 18¼)"
31 (33, 36, 38, 42, 46.5) cm

8¼ (8½, 9 9¼, 9¾, 10½)"
21 (21.5, 23, 23.5, 25, 26.5) cm

17 (17½, 17½, 18, 18, 18)"
43 (44.5, 44.5, 45.5, 45.5, 45.5) cm

17"
43 cm

6¾ (7¼, 7½, 8, 8½, 8¾)"
17 (18.5, 19, 20.5, 21.5, 22) cm

4¾"
12 cm

33 (36¾, 40¾, 44½, 48½, 52½)"
84 (93.5, 103.5, 113, 123, 133.5) cm
with 2 (2, 2½, 2¼, 2¼, 2¼)"
5 (5, 6.5, 5.5, 5.5, 5.5) cm gap

36¾ (40¾, 44½, 48½, 52½, 56¼)"
93.5 (103.5, 113, 123, 133.5, 143) cm
with 2 (2, 2½, 2¼, 2¼, 2¼)"
5 (5, 6.5, 5.5, 5.5, 5.5) cm gap

Sleeve dec row 1: (RS) *Work in established patt to armhole m, sl m, k2tog, knit to 2 sts before next armhole m, ssk, sl m; rep from * once more, then work to end of row—4 sts dec'd.

Work 2 rows even.

Sleeve dec row 2: (WS) *Work in established patt to armhole m, sl m, ssp, purl to 2 sts before next armhole m, p2tog, sl m; rep from * once more, then work to end of row—4 sts dec'd.

Work 2 rows even.

Rep last 6 rows 4 more times—194 (202, 206, 206, 210, 214) sts rem, with 25 (25, 23, 21, 21, 21) sts for each sleeve, 36 (38, 40, 41, 42, 43) sts for each front, and 72 (76, 80, 82, 84, 86) sts for back.

Next sleeve dec row: (RS) Rep Sleeve dec row 1—4 sts dec'd.

Next sleeve dec row: (WS) Rep Sleeve dec row 2—4 sts dec'd.

Cont sleeve dec every row 4 (4, 3, 2, 2, 2) more times—170 (178, 186, 190, 194, 198) sts rem, with 13 sts for each sleeve, 36 (38, 40, 41, 42, 43) sts for each front, and 72 (76, 80, 82, 84, 86) sts for back.

Work 0 (0, 1, 0, 0, 0) row(s) even.

Next row: (RS) Work in patt to m, remove m, CO 1 st using the backward-loop method (see Glossary), place these 31 sts onto holder and do not break yarn.

RIGHT FRONT SHOULDER

Next row: (RS) Knit to armhole m, sl m, ssk, turn—1 st dec'd at sleeve cap.

Next row: (WS) Sl 1 pwise, purl to end of row.

Rep last 2 rows 4 more times—7 (9, 11, 12, 13, 14) sts rem for right front shoulder. Place sts onto holder. Cut yarn, leaving long tail for joining shoulders.

RIGHT BACK SHOULDER

Next row: (RS) Join MC to right sleeve cap, k2tog, knit to armhole m, sl m, k6 (8, 10, 11, 12, 13), turn—1 st dec'd at sleeve cap.

Next row: (WS) Purl to armhole m, sl m, p2tog, turn—1 st dec'd at sleeve cap.

Next row: (RS) Sl 1 pwise, knit to end of row.

Rep last 2 rows 4 more times—7 (9, 11, 12, 13, 14) sts rem for right back shoulder. Place sts onto holder.

BO next 60 sts for back neck.

LEFT BACK SHOULDER

Next row: (RS) Knit 5 (7, 9, 10, 11, 12) more sts (6 [8, 10, 11, 12, 13] sts on right needle tip after BO), sl m, ssk, turn—1 st dec'd at sleeve cap.

Next row: (WS) Sl 1 pwise, sl m, purl to end of row.

Next row: (RS) Knit to armhole m, sl m, ssk, turn—1 st dec'd at sleeve cap.

Next row: (WS) Sl 1 pwise, sl m, purl to end of row.

Rep last 2 rows 3 more times—7 (9, 11, 12, 13, 14) sts rem for left back shoulder. Place sts onto holder. Cut yarn, leaving long tail for joining shoulders.

LEFT FRONT SHOULDER

Next row: (RS) Join MC to left sleeve cap, k2tog, knit to armhole m, sl m, knit to end of row—1 st dec'd at sleeve cap.

Next row: (WS) Purl to armhole m, sl m, p2tog, turn—1 st dec'd at sleeve cap.

Next row: (RS) Sl 1 pwise, knit to end of row.

Rep last 2 rows 4 more times—7 (9, 11, 12, 13, 14) sts rem for left front shoulder. Place sts onto holder. Cut yarn.

Remove m and with CC, CO 1 st using the backward-loop method, then work to end of row—31 sts. Place sts onto holder but do not cut yarn.

Graft shoulders tog using Kitchener st (see Glossary).

Collar

Return 31 held sts for left front band to larger cir needle.

Cont in established patt, working CO st in Garter st until band reaches center of back neck. Place sts onto holder.

Rep with right front band.

Finishing

Graft underarm seams tog using Kitchener st (see Glossary).

Graft left and right front bands tog using Kitchener st. Sew collar to back neck.

HEM

Carefully remove provisional CO and place sts onto smaller cir needle.

Next row: (RS) Join MC and work in St st for 1" (2.5 cm), ending with a WS row.

BO all sts. Cut yarn, leaving long tail at least 3 times longer than bottom width.

Fold hem to WS, and using long tail, sew BO edge to body. If desired, use same tail or other yarn tails to sew each side of hem to side of front bands.

Weave in ends. Block to measurements.

Fold collar to RS for desired shawl collar appearance and tack in place at center back, tops of shoulders, and front neck with CC.

Using matching sewing thread, sew toggles to front edges below shawl collar.

SLIP-STITCH *cowl*

This easy knit only looks complex due to a simple slip-stitch pattern worked with two gradient yarns. The complementary colors merge to create a dazzling colorplay. Pairing a warm gradient with a cool one causes both colorways to pop. The design uses less than two balls of yarn, so for a wider cowl, just cast on additional stitches in multiples of four. • **Caroline Dick**

FINISHED SIZE
About 27" (68.5 cm)
circumference and
13¾" (35 cm) long.

YARN
Fingering weight
(#1 Super Fine).

Shown here: KnitCircus
Yarns Opulence (80%
superwash merino
wool, 10% cashmere,
10% nylon; 440 yd

[402 m]/3½ oz [100g]):
A Kid in a Candy Store
(A), 1 ball; Happy
Little Trees (B), 1 ball.

NEEDLES
Size U.S. 3 (3.25 mm):
24" (60 cm)
circular (cir).

*Adjust needle size if
necessary to obtain
the correct gauge.*

NOTIONS
Marker (m);
tapestry needle.

GAUGE
29½ sts and 46
rows = 4" (10 cm)
in Slip St patt.

NOTE
• If you are making a
shorter cowl or want
the color to change
faster, break the
yarn and remove a
section of yarn, rejoin,
then continue.

**Slip-Stitch Pattern
(multiple of 4 sts)**

Rnd 1: With A, knit.

Rnds 2–4: With B, *k3, sl 1 wyb; rep from * to end of rnd.

Rnd 5: With B, knit.

Rnds 6–8: With A, *k3, sl 1 wyb; rep from * to end of rnd.

Rep Rnds 1–8 for patt.

P3, K1 Rib (multiple of 4 sts)

All rnds: *P3, k1; rep from * to end of rnd.

Cowl

With A, CO 200 sts. Place marker (pm) and join for working in rnds, being careful not to twist sts.

Work in p3, k1 rib (see Stitch Guide) for 10 rnds.

Work Rnds 1–8 of slip st patt (see Stitch Guide) 17 times, or to desired length, ending with Rnd 8. Cut A.

With B, knit 1 rnd.

Work in p3, k1 rib for 10 rnds. BO all sts in ribbing.

Finishing

Weave in ends. Block to measurements.

REVERSIBLE BRIOCHE
infinity scarf

Switching between brioche knit and brioche purl mid-row results in a two-tone, vertically striped, reversible cowl. One column of color is held constant and serves as an anchor for the color play of shifting hues in the other column. I-cord edges add a neat finish. • **Carolyn Bloom**

FINISHED SIZE
About 9½" (24 cm) wide and 48½" (123 cm) long.

YARN
Fingering Weight (#1 Super Fine).

Shown here: Spun Right Round Classic Sock (100% superwash merino wool; 438 yd [401 m]/3½ oz [100 g]): Pavement (C1), 1 skein; Idle Gossip (C2), 1 skein; The Water's Fine (C3), 1 skein; Reaper's Rages (MC), 1 skein.

NEEDLES
Size U.S. 2 (2.75 mm): 24" (60 cm) circular (cir).

Size U.S. 5 (3.75 mm): double-pointed (dpn).

Adjust needle size if necessary to obtain the correct gauge.

NOTIONS
Size F (3.75 mm) crochet hook; waste yarn; markers (m); tapestry needle.

GAUGE
26 sts and 33 rows = 4" (10 cm) in brioche st on smaller needles, blocked.

NOTES
• Gauge is not critical for this project, but deviating from these measurements may effect yardage requirements, particularly for the MC.

• This pattern calls for a tight brioche stitch; block gently to achieve an ideal drape. When blocking brioche, pin the piece to the desired measurements and spray with water or water with a drop or two of wool wash. The finished measurements for the cowl were achieved using this technique. If you fully submerge your piece, these dimensions may be difficult to obtain.

• There are no right and wrong sides to this piece, but for ease in working the two-color brioche rib, odd-numbered rows are designated as RS rows, and even-numbered rows are designated as WS rows.

Brk (brioche knit):

Knit the stitch together with its accompanying yarnover.

Brp (brioche purl):

Purl the stitch together with its accompanying yarnover.

Yf sl1yo (yarn forward, slip 1, yarnover):

Bring yarn forward, slip 1 purlwise, bring yarn over right needle.

I-Cord (3 sts)

Row 1: K3. Do not turn.

Row 2: Without turning the needle, slide sts to other end of needle, pull yarn around the back and k3. Do not turn.

Rep Row 2 for I-cord.

Cowl

I-CORD FOUNDATION

Using crochet hook and waste yarn, provisionally cast 3 sts onto dpn (see Glossary).

Join C1. Work I-cord for 59 rows (see Stitch Guide).

Change to cir needle. Join MC.

With MC, work 1 more I-cord row, skip 1 I-cord row, pick up and knit 58 sts along side of I-cord (1 st in each row), ending 1 row before provisional cast-on. Bring MC to the front of work.

> **NOTE** One I-cord row will be skipped between the picked-up sts and the provisional CO.

Remove provisional CO and place these 3 sts onto right needle tip with purl bumps facing—64 sts.

Slide sts to other end of needle. Do not turn work.

Join C1.

Set-up row: (WS) With C1 and working set-up row of chart, k3, [yf sl1yo, k1] 14 times, yf sl1yo, place marker (pm), [yf sl1yo, p1] 14 times, yf sl1yo, [sl wyf] 3 times. Turn work.

Row 1: (MC, RS) Working row 1 (MC) of chart, k3, [brp, yf sl1yo] 14 times, brp, sl m, [brk, yf sl1yo] 14 times, brk, [sl wyf] 3 times. Slide sts to other end of needle. Do not turn.

Row 1: (CC, RS) Working row 1 (CC) of chart, k3, [yf sl1yo, brk] 14 times, yf sl1yo, sl m, [yf sl1yo, brp] 14 times, yf sl1yo, [sl wyf] 3 times. Turn work.

Row 2: (MC, WS) Working row 2 (MC) of chart, k3, brp, [yf sl1yo, brp] 14 times, sl m, brk, [yf sl1yo, brk] 14 times, [sl wyf] 3 times. Slide sts to other end of needle. Do not turn.

BRIOCHE CHART

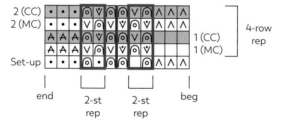

2 (CC)
2 (MC)

1 (CC)
1 (MC)

4-row rep

Set-up

end
2-st rep
2-st rep
beg

☐ MC

▨ CC

☐ k on RS rows, p on WS rows

• p on RS rows, k on WS rows

⊙ yf sl1yo (see Stitch Guide)

V brk on RS, brp on WS (see Stitch Guide)

V brp on RS, brk on WS (see Stitch Guide)

∧ sl 1 wyf on WS

A sl 1 wyf on RS

| marker

☐ pattern repeat

Row 2: (CC, WS) K3, yf sl1yo, [brk, yf sl1yo] 14 times, sl m, yf sl1yo, [brp, yf sl1yo] 14 times, [sl wyf] 3 times. Turn work.

> **NOTE** When working with CC, you will need to work "yf sl1yo" on either side of the marker. To do so, work "yf sl1yo" once, slip the marker, return yarn to front of work and do second "yf sl1yo."

Rep Rows 1 (MC) to 2 (CC) 15 more times.

> **TIP** When working with MC, you will always work your brioche stitches as brp in the first half of the row and as brk in the second half of the row. When working with CC, you will always work your brioche stitches as brk in the first half of the row and as brp in the second half of the row. Once the color blocks have been established, this will become intuitive.

COLOR SHIFT 1

Shift to next contrasting color as foll.

Cont working the MC half of each row as established, work the CC half of each row: [2 rows with C2, 4 rows with C1] twice, [2 rows with C2, 2 rows with C1] 3 times, [4 rows with C2, 2 rows with C1] twice—total of 36 rows worked. Cut C1.

Work Rows 1 (MC) to 2 (CC) of brioche patt 32 times using MC and C2.

COLOR SHIFT 2

Cont working the MC half of each row as established, work the CC half of each row: [2 rows with C3, 4 rows with C2] twice, [2 rows with C3, 2 rows with C2] 3 times, [4 rows with C3, 2 rows with C2] twice—total of 36 rows worked. Cut C2.

Work Rows 1 (MC) to 2 (CC) of brioche patt 32 times using MC and C3.

COLOR SHIFT 3

Cont working the MC half of each row as established, work the CC half of each row: [2 rows with C2, 4 rows with C3] twice, [2 rows with C2, 2 rows with C3] 3 times, [4 rows with C2, 2 rows with C3] twice—total of 36 rows worked. Cut C3.

Work Rows 1 (MC) to 2 (CC) of brioche patt 32 times using MC and C2.

COLOR SHIFT 4

Cont working the MC half of each row as established, work the CC half of each row: [2 rows with C1, 4 rows with C2] twice, [2 rows with C1, 2 rows with C2] 3 times, [4 rows with C1, 2 rows with C2] twice—total of 36 rows worked. Cut C2.

Work Rows 1 (MC) to 2 (CC) of brioche patt 16 times using MC and C1.

I-CORD BIND-OFF

With dpn, k3. Do not turn. Sl these sts back to left needle.

BO row: (RS) Using dpn, *k2, k2tog tbl (third stitch of I-cord with next stitch of cowl). Do not turn. Sl these sts back to left needle tip; rep from * until 6 sts rem (3 edge sts and 3 I-cord sts).

> **NOTE** Make sure to treat the slipped stitches and paired yo's as 1 stitch when joining the I-cord.

Turning the Corner

Next row: K3, but do not slide sts to other end of dpn. Cut MC, leaving a 9" (23 cm) tail. Rearrange I-cord sts to line up with rem sts on LH needle by firmly grasping sts at their bases, remove dpn and reinsert into sts from opposite direction. Join I-cord BO sts to rem 3 sts using Kitchener st (see Glossary).

Finishing

Cut CC, leaving a 25" (63.5 cm) tail. Use CC to sew center st of I-cord BO together with center st of I-cord foundation.

Weave in ends. Block if desired (if you are going to block your cowl, it will be easier to do so before sewing the ends together).

SPECTRUM *hat*

Working with two sets of four gradient yarns
offers endless opportunity for creativity in this stranded
cap. Several design elements manipulate the intensity
of the colors. As the background stripes reduce in size,
the foreground pattern height increases. And the lighter
color in one gradient is paired with the darkest in
the other. It adds up to a sophisticated rainbow
of glorious color! • **Kyle Kunnecke**

FINISHED SIZE

About 16¼" (41.5 cm) circumference above brim and 8½" (21.5 cm) long.

YARN

Sock weight (#1 Super Fine).

Shown here: SweetGeorgia Yarns Tough Love Party of Five Mini-Skein Set (80% merino wool, 20% nylon; 525 yd [480 m]/5 oz [142 g]): Wildfire, 1 pack; Sea to Sky, 1 pack.

Only four of the five colors in each pack are used. Label the colors used as follows: from Wildfire pack, Cayenne (A), Pumpkin (B), Dutch (C), and Saffron (D); from Sea to Sky pack, Salt Air (E), Evergreen (F), Fern (G), and Basil (H).

NEEDLES

Size U.S. 1 (2.5 mm): 16" (40 cm) circular (cir) or double-pointed (dpn).

Size U.S. 2 (2.75 mm): 16" (40 cm) cir and dpn.

Adjust needle size if necessary to obtain the correct gauge.

NOTIONS

Markers (m), one in unique color for beginning of rnd; tapestry needle.

GAUGE

34½ sts and 39 rnds = 4" (10 cm) in stranded pattern with larger needles.

NOTES

• Weaving in ends as you go will simplify finishing later. Remember to weave ends in on stitches of the same color when possible.

• Trim tails to 1" (2.5 cm) and wait until after final blocking to make the final trim.

Hat

With A and smaller cir needle, CO 140 sts. Place maker (pm) in unique color and join for working in rnds, being careful not to twist sts.

Next rnd: *K1, p1; rep from * to end of rnd.

Rep last rnd until piece measures 1" (2.5 cm) from beg.

Next rnd: [K10, pm] 13 times, k10.

Change to larger cir needle. Join E.

Next rnd: Reading Color chart from right to left, *work Rnd 1 of chart over 10 sts; rep from * 13 more times.

Work Rnds 2–73 of chart as established, change colors as indicated—14 sts rem. Cut E.

COLOR CHART

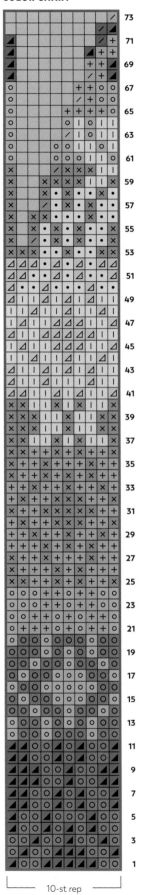

10-st rep

NOTE *Change to dpn when there are too few sts on cir needle to work comfortably.*

Next (dec) rnd: With B, [k2tog] around—7 sts rem. Cut yarn, leaving a 10" (25.5 cm) tail, thread tail through rem sts, pulling tightly to close hole, and fasten off on WS.

Finishing

Weave in rem ends. Wet-block. Trim rem ends.

○	A
+	B
ı	C
•	D
◣	E
○	F
×	G
◢	H
╱	k2tog
	no stitch
☐	pattern repeat

DYE-AGONAL STRIPES *cardigan*

Two sets of vibrant colors flow into each other in this bottom-up cardigan that has set-in sleeves and a simple, flattering shape. The diagonal stripe pattern is easy to memorize, while remaining entertaining as the colors progress, and is suitable for beginner and intermediate colorwork knitters. • **Megan Dial**

FINISHED SIZES
About 34¾ (38½, 42¾, 46½)" (88.5 [98, 108.5, 118] cm) bust circumference and 29¾" (75.5 cm) long.

Cardigan shown measures 34¾" (88.5 cm).

YARN
Sportweight (#2 Fine).

Shown here: Frabjous Fibers Wonderland Mini Skein Packs Mad Hatter Sport So Fond of Rainbows (100% superwash merino wool; 1,720 yd [1,573 m]/20 oz [567 g]): Enchanted Woodland, 1 (2, 2, 2) pack(s).

Each pack consists of twenty mini skeins; each skein is 86 yd [79 m]/1 oz [28.35 g].

NEEDLES
Size U.S. 7 (4.5mm): 24" and 40" (60 and 100 cm) circular (cir).

Adjust needle size if necessary to obtain the correct gauge.

NOTIONS
Markers (m); tapestry needle.

GAUGE
26 sts and 24 rows = 4" (10 cm) in Diagonal patt.

NOTE
• Separate the colors into two 10-color gradient sets. Label the balls in the first set A1–A10 from dark to light and in the second set B1–B10 from light to dark.

K2, P2 Rib
(multiple of 4 sts + 2)

Row 1: (RS) *K2, p2; rep from * to last 2 sts, k2.

Row 2: (WS) P2, *k2, p2; rep from * to end of row.

Rep Rows 1 and 2 for patt.

Diagonal Pattern
(multiple of 4 sts + 2)

Row 1: (RS) *K2 in A, k2 in B; rep from * to last 2 sts, k2 in A.

Row 2: (WS) P1 in A, *p2 in B, p2 in A; rep from * to last st, p1 in B.

Row 3: *K2 in B, k2 in A; rep from * to last 2 sts, k2 in B.

Row 4: P1 in B, *p2 in A, p2 in B; rep from * to last st, p1 in A.

Rep Rows 1–4 for patt.

Body Stripe Pattern

Working in Diagonal patt, work 10 rows with A2 and B2, ending with a WS row. Cut A2.

Join A3, and work 10 rows in Diagonal patt, ending with a WS row. Cut B2.

Join B3, and work 10 rows in Diagonal patt, ending with a WS row. Cut A3.

Join A4, and work 10 rows in Diagonal patt, ending with a WS row. Cut B3.

Join B4, and work 10 rows in Diagonal patt, ending with a WS row. Cut A4.

Join A5, and work 10 rows in Diagonal patt, ending with a WS row. Cut B4.

Join B5, and work 10 rows in Diagonal patt, ending with a WS row. Cut A5.

Join A6, and work 10 rows in Diagonal patt, ending with a WS row. Cut B5.

Join B6, and work 10 rows in Diagonal patt, ending with a WS row. Cut A6.

Join A7, and work 10 rows in Diagonal patt, ending with a WS row. Cut B6.

Join B7, and work 10 rows in Diagonal patt, ending with a WS row. Cut A7.

Join A8, and work 10 rows in Diagonal patt, ending with a WS row. Cut B7.

Join B8, and work 10 rows in Diagonal patt, ending with a WS row. Cut A8.

Join A9, and work 10 rows in Diagonal patt, ending with a WS row. Cut B8.

Join B9, and work 10 rows in Diagonal patt, ending with a WS row. Cut A9.

Join A10, and work 10 rows in Diagonal patt, ending with a WS row. Cut B9.

Join B10, and work to end with A10 and B10.

Sleeve Stripe Pattern

Work 8 rows with A2 and B2. Cut A2.

Join A3. Cont same as Body Stripe patt, changing to next A or B color every 8 rows.

Body

With longer cir needle and A1, CO 210 (234, 262, 286) sts. Cut yarn.

Rows 1–4: Join B1, and work k2, p2 rib, ending with a WS row. Cut yarn.

Rows 5–8: Join A1, and work in k2, p2 rib, ending with a WS row. Cut yarn.

Join A2 and B2. Beg diagonal patt (see Stitch Guide or chart) and body stripe patt (see Stitch Guide), and work until piece measures about 19¾" (50 cm) from beg.

DIAGONAL PATTERN

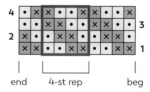

| end | 4-st rep | beg |

☒ A
· B
☐ pattern repeat

SHAPE FRONT NECK

Place markers (pm) 50 (55, 63, 68) sts from each end of row for fronts, with 110 (124, 136, 150) sts between m for back.

Dec row: (RS) Cont in patt, k1, ssk, work to last 3 sts, k2tog, k1—2 sts dec'd.

Cont changing colors every 10 rows as established, rep Dec row every RS row 6 (6, 10, 10) more times, then every 4 rows 3 times. At the same time, when 10 (8, 4, 2) more rows have been worked, end with a WS row. Piece should measure about 21½ (21, 20½, 20)" (54.5 [53.5, 52, 51] cm) from beg.

DIVIDE FOR FRONTS AND BACK

Next row: (RS) Cont front neck dec, and established patt, *work to 5 (6, 7, 9) sts before m, BO 10 (12, 14, 18) sts for armhole; rep from * once more, then work to end of row—39 (44, 53, 57) sts rem for each front, and 100 (112, 122, 132) sts rem for back. Place 39 (44, 53, 57) sts for left front onto shorter cir needle and leave back and right front sts on hold on longer cir needle.

LEFT FRONT
Shape Armhole
Work 1 WS row even.

Armhole dec row 1: (RS) Cont in est patt, k1, [ssk] twice, then work to end of row—2 sts dec'd at armhole.

Rep last 2 rows 1 (1, 2, 2) more time(s)—2 (2, 4, 4) sts dec'd at armhole.

Work 1 row even.

Armhole dec row 2: (RS) K1, ssk, then work to end of row—1 st dec'd at armhole.

back & front

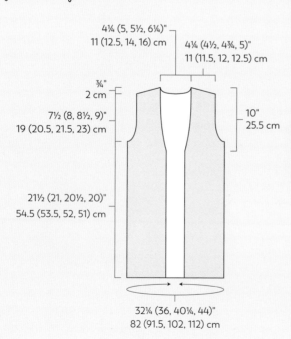

4¼ (5, 5½, 6¼)"
11 (12.5, 14, 16) cm

4¼ (4½, 4¾, 5)"
11 (11.5, 12, 12.5) cm

¾"
2 cm

7½ (8, 8½, 9)"
19 (20.5, 21.5, 23) cm

10"
25.5 cm

21½ (21, 20½, 20)"
54.5 (53.5, 52, 51) cm

32¼ (36, 40¼, 44)"
82 (91.5, 102, 112) cm

sleeve

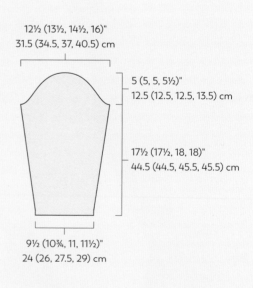

12½ (13½, 14½, 16)"
31.5 (34.5, 37, 40.5) cm

5 (5, 5, 5½)"
12.5 (12.5, 12.5, 13.5) cm

17½ (17½, 18, 18)"
44.5 (44.5, 45.5, 45.5) cm

9½ (10¾, 11, 11½)"
24 (26, 27.5, 29) cm

Rep last 2 rows 3 (5, 4, 6) more times—27 (29, 31, 32) sts rem when all shaping is complete.

Cont even in established patt until 10 rows have been worked with A10 and 20 rows have been worked with B9, ending with a WS row. Cut B9.

Join B10, and work 6 rows in patt, ending with a WS row. Armhole should measure about 7½ (8, 8½, 9)" (19 [20.5, 21.5, 23] cm).

Shape Shoulder
BO 9 (10, 10, 11) sts at beg of next 2 RS rows—9 (9, 11, 10) sts rem.

BO rem sts on next row.

BACK
Shape Armholes
Next row: (WS) Join appropriate A and B colors at left armhole and work 1 row even.

Dec row 1: (RS) Cont in patt, k1, [ssk] twice, work to last 5 sts, [k2tog] twice, k1—4 sts dec'd.

Rep last 2 rows 1 (1, 2, 2) more time(s)—92 (104, 110, 120) sts rem.

Work 1 row even.

Dec row 2: K1, ssk, work to last 3 sts, k2tog, k1—2 sts dec'd.

Rep last 2 rows 4 (6, 5, 7) more times—82 (90, 98, 104) sts rem.

Cont even until 10 rows of A9 and 20 rows of B8 have been worked, ending with a WS row. Cut B8.

Join B9, and work 10 rows in patt, ending with a WS row. Cut A9. Wind off about 10 yd (9 m) of A10 and set aside for shoulder.

Join A10, and work 10 rows in patt, ending with a WS row. Cut B9. Wind off about 10 yd (9 m) of B10 and set aside for shoulder.

Join B10, and work 4 rows in patt, ending with a WS row. Armholes should measure about 7 (7½, 8, 8½)" (18 [19, 20.5, 21.5] cm).

Shape Back Neck & Shoulders

Pm each side of center 20 (24, 28, 32) sts for neck.

Next row: (RS) Work to m, join reserved balls of A10 and B10 and BO marked sts in patt, then work to end of row—31 (33, 35, 36) sts rem each shoulder. Cont each side separately.

Next row: (WS) Work to neck edge; BO 2 sts, then work to end of row.

Next row: BO 9 (10, 10, 11) sts, work to neck edge; BO 2 sts, then work to end of row.

Next row: BO 9 (10, 10, 11) sts, work to neck edge; BO 1 st, then work to end of row.

Next row: BO 9 (10, 10, 11) sts, work to neck edge; BO 1 st, then work to end of row.

Next row: BO 9 (10, 10, 11) sts, work to neck edge; BO 1 st, then work to end of row.

Next row: BO rem 9 (9, 11, 10) sts; BO 1 st, then work to end of row.

Next row: BO rem 9 (9, 11, 10) sts.

RIGHT FRONT

Shape Armhole

Next row: (WS) Join appropriate A and B colors at armhole and work 1 row even.

Armhole dec row 1: (RS) Cont in established patt, work to last 5 sts, [k2tog] twice, k1—2 sts dec'd at armhole.

Rep last 2 rows 1 (1, 2, 2) more time(s)—2 (2, 4, 4) sts dec'd at armhole.

Work 1 row even.

Armhole dec row 2: (RS) Work to last 3 sts, k2tog, k1—1 st dec'd at armhole.

Rep last 2 rows 3 (5, 4, 6) more times—27 (29, 31, 32) sts rem when all shaping is complete.

Cont even until 10 rows in A10 and 20 rows in B9 have been worked, ending with a WS row. Cut B9.

Join B10, and work 5 rows in patt, ending with a RS row. Armhole should measure about 7½ (8, 8½, 9)" (19 [20.5, 21.5, 23] cm).

Shape Shoulder

BO 9 (10, 10, 11) sts at beg of next 2 WS rows—9 (9, 11, 10) sts rem.

BO rem sts on next row.

Sleeves

With shorter cir needle and A1, CO 62 (66, 70, 74) sts. Cut yarn.

Rows 1–4: Join B1, and work 4 rows in k2, p2 rib, ending with a WS row. Cut yarn.

Rows 5–8: Join A1, and work 4 rows in k2, p2 rib, ending with a WS row. Cut yarn.

Join A2 and B2. Beg diagonal patt and sleeve stripe patt (see Stitch Guide), work 16 (10, 12, 8) rows even, ending with a WS row.

Inc row: (RS) Cont in patt, k1, M1, work to last st, M1, k1—2 sts inc'd.

Rep Inc row every 8 (8, 6, 6) rows 9 (10, 6, 14) more times, then every 0 (0, 8, 0) rows 0 (0, 5, 0) times—82 (88, 94, 104) sts.

Cont even until piece measures 17½ (17½, 18, 18)" (44.5 [44.5, 45.5, 45.5] cm) from beg, ending with a WS row.

SHAPE CAP

BO 5 (6, 7, 9) sts at beg of next 2 rows, 4 sts at beg of next 0 (0, 2, 2) rows, 3 sts at beg of next 2 rows, then 2 sts at beg of next 6 (6, 4, 4) rows—54 (58, 58, 64) sts rem.

Dec row: (RS) K1, ssk, work to last 3 sts, k2tog, k1—2 sts dec'd.

Rep Dec row every RS row 3 (3, 3, 4) more times—46 (50, 50, 54) sts rem.

BO 2 sts at beg of next 8 (6, 8, 6) rows, 3 sts at beg of next 2 (4, 2, 4) rows, then 4 sts at beg of next 2 rows—16 (18, 20, 22) sts rem.

BO rem sts in patt.

Finishing

Weave in ends. Block pieces to measurements.

Sew shoulder seams.

NECKBAND

With longer cir needle, A1, and with RS facing, pick up and knit 178 sts evenly along right front edge, 42 (46, 50, 54) sts along back neck, then 178 sts along left front—398 (402, 406, 410) sts. Do not join.

Beg with a WS row, work 4 rows in k2, p2 rib, ending with a RS row. Cut yarn.

Join B1, and work 5 rows in k2, p2 rib, ending with a WS row. Cut yarn.

Join A1 and BO all sts loosely in patt.

Sew sleeve seams. Set in sleeves.

abbreviations

beg	begin; beginning	**LH**	left hand	**sl**	slip
BO	bind off	**m(s)**	marker(s)	**ssk**	slip, slip, knit
C	color	**M1L**	make 1 left	**ssp**	slip, slip, purl
CC	contrasting color	**M1R**	make 1 right	**St st**	stockinette stitch
cir	circular	**MC**	main color	**st(s)**	stitch(es)
cn	cable needle	**p**	purl	**tbl**	through the back loop
CO	cast on	**p2tog**	purl 2 stitches together	**tog**	together
cont	continue(s); continuing	**patt(s)**	pattern(s)	**WS**	wrong side
dec('d)	decrease(s)('d); decreasing	**pm**	place marker	**wyb**	with yarn in back
dpn	double-pointed needle(s)	**psso**	pass slipped stitch over	**wyf**	with yarn in front
foll	following; follows	**pwise**	purlwise	**yo**	yarn over
inc('d)	increase(s)('d); increasing	**rem**	remain(s); remaining	*****	repeat starting point
k	knit	**rep**	repeat; repeating	******	repeat all instructions between asterisks
k1f&b	knit into front and back of same st	**RH**	right hand	**( )**	alternate measurements and/ or instructions
k2tog	knit 2 stitches together	**rnd(s)**	round(s)	**[ ]**	instructions that are to be worked as a group a specified number of times
kwise	knitwise	**RS**	right side		
		sk2p	slip 1, knit 2 stitches together, pass slipped stitch over		

glossary

Cast-Ons

LONG-TAIL CAST-ON

Leaving a long tail (about 1–2" for each stitch to be cast on), make a slipknot and place on right needle. Place thumb and index finger of left hand between yarn ends so that working yarn is around index finger and tail end is around thumb. Secure ends with your other fingers and hold palm upwards, making a V of yarn **(Figure 1)**. Bring needle up through loop on thumb **(Figure 2)**, grab first strand around index finger with needle, and go back down through loop on thumb **(Figure 3)**. Drop loop off thumb and, placing thumb back in V configuration, tighten resulting stitch on needle **(Figure 4)**.

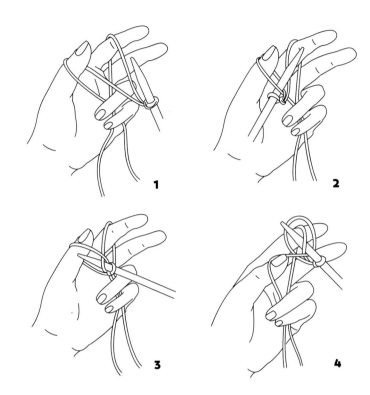

PROVISIONAL CAST-ON

Place a loose slipknot on needle held in your right hand. Hold waste yarn next to slipknot and around left thumb; hold working yarn over left index finger. *Bring needle forward under waste yarn, over working yarn, grab a loop of working yarn **(Figure 1)**, then bring needle to the front, over both yarns, and grab a second loop **(Figure 2)**. Repeat from *. When you're ready to use the cast-on stitches, pick out waste yarn to expose live stitches.

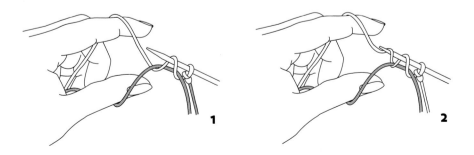

Cast-Ons, cont'd

CROCHET PROVISIONAL CAST-ON

With smooth contrasting waste yarn and crochet hook, make a loose chain of about four stitches more than you need to cast on. Cut yarn and pull tail through last chain to secure. With needle, working yarn, and beginning two stitches from last chain worked, pick up and knit one stitch through the back loop of each chain **(Figure 1)** for desired number of stitches. Work the piece as desired, and when you're ready to use the cast-on stitches, pull out the crochet chain to expose the live stitches **(Figure 2)**.

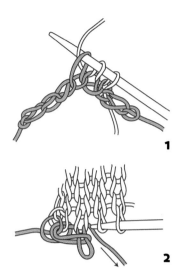

CABLE CAST-ON

If there are no established stitches, begin with a slipknot, knit one stitch in slipknot and slip this new stitch to left needle. *Insert right needle between first two stitches on left needle **(Figure 1)**. Wrap yarn as if to knit. Draw yarn through to complete stitch **(Figure 2)** and slip this new stitch to left needle as shown **(Figure 3)**. Repeat from *.

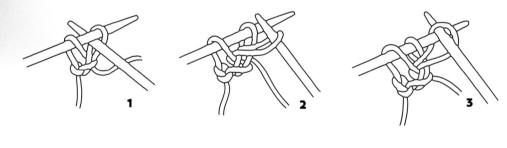

KNITTED CAST-ON

Place slipknot on left needle if there are no established stitches. *With right needle, knit into first stitch (or slipknot) on left needle **(Figure 1)** and place new stitch onto left needle **(Figure 2)**. Repeat from *, always knitting into last stitch made.

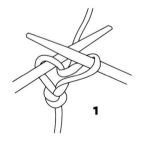
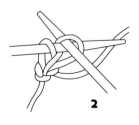

BACKWARD-LOOP CAST-ON

*Loop working yarn as shown and place it on needle backward (with right leg of loop in back of needle). Repeat from *.

Bind-Offs

STANDARD BIND-OFF

Knit the first stitch, *knit the next stitch (two stitches on the right needle), insert left needle tip into first stitch on the right needle **(Figure 1)** and lift this stitch up and over the second stitch **(Figure 2)** and off the needle **(Figure 3)**. Repeat from * for the desired number of stitches.

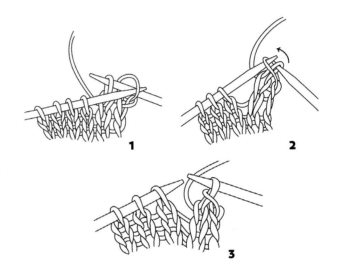

THREE-NEEDLE BIND-OFF

Place the stitches to be joined onto two separate needles and hold the needles parallel so that the right sides (or wrong sides, if specified in pattern) of knitting face together. Insert a third needle into the first stitch on each of two needles **(Figure 1)** and knit them together as one stitch **(Figure 2)**, *knit the next stitch on each needle the same way, then use the left needle tip to lift the first stitch over the second and off the needle **(Figure 3)**. Repeat from * until no stitches remain on the first two needles. Cut yarn and pull tail through last stitch to secure.

Bind-Offs, cont'd

JENY'S SURPRISINGLY STRETCHY BIND-OFF

To Collar a Knit Stitch: Bring working yarn from back to front over needle in the opposite direction of a normal yarnover **(Figure 1)**, knit the next stitch, then lift the yarnover over the top of the knitted stitch and off the needle **(Figure 2)**.

To Collar a Purl Stitch: Bring working yarn from front to back over needle as for a normal yarnover **(Figure 3)**, purl the next stitch, then lift the yarnover over the top of the purled stitch and off the needle **(Figure 4)**.

To begin, collar each of the first two stitches to match their knit or purl nature. Then pass the first collared stitch over the second and off the right needle—one stitch is bound off.

*Collar the next stitch according to its nature **(Figure 5)**, then pass the previous stitch over the collared stitch and off the needle **(Figure 6)**.

Repeat from * until one stitch remains on the right needle. Cut the yarn, leaving a 6" (15 cm) tail, then pull on the loop of the last stitch until the tail comes free.

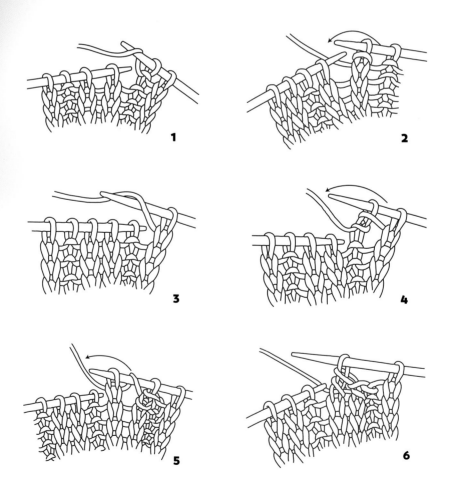

Increases

MAKE ONE (M1) INCREASES

This increase makes a stitch out of the horizontal "ladder" that extends between every two stitches. This is a subtle increase that can slant either to the right or left, depending on the way you work the horizontal ladder.

NOTE *Use the left slant (M1L) if no direction is specified. For the purl versions (M1P, M1LP, and M1RP), work as for the knit versions, purling the lifted loop.*

Left-Slant (M1L) and Standard M1

With left needle tip, lift strand between needles from front to back **(Figure 1)**. Knit lifted loop through the back **(Figure 2)**.

Right-Slant (M1R)

With left needle tip, lift strand between needles from back to front **(Figure 1)**. Knit lifted loop through the front **(Figure 2)**.

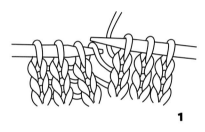

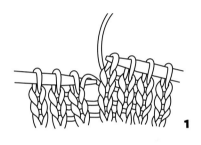

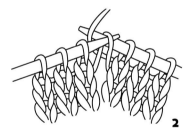

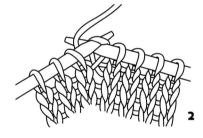

KNIT 1 INTO FRONT AND BACK (K1F&B)

Knit into a stitch and leave it on the needle **(Figure 1)**. Knit through the back loop of the same stitch **(Figure 2)**. Slip both stitches off the needle **(Figure 3)**.

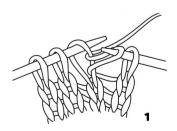

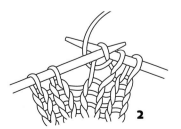

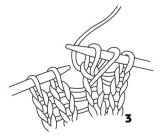

Decreases

KNIT 2 TOGETHER (K2TOG)

Insert the right needle into two stitches (at the same time) knitwise and knit them as if they were a single stitch.

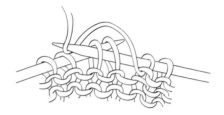

PURL 2 TOGETHER (P2TOG)

Purl two stitches together as if they were a single stitch.

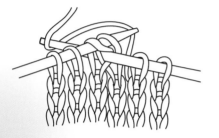

SLIP, SLIP, KNIT (SSK)

Slip two stitches knitwise one at a time (**Figure 1**). Insert point of left needle into front of two slipped stitches and knit them together through back loops with right needle (**Figure 2**).

LEFT-SLANT DOUBLE DECREASE (SK2P)

Slip one stitch knitwise (**Figure 1**), then k2tog (**Figure 2**). Insert the left needle into the second stitch on the right needle and pass this stitch over the first stitch (**Figure 3**)—two stitches decreased.

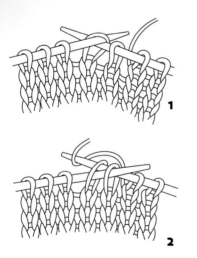

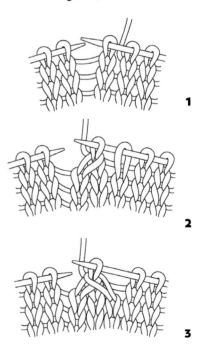

KNIT 2 TOGETHER THROUGH THE BACK LOOP (K2TOG TBL)

Insert needle into back loop of two stitches and knit together as if they were a single stitch.

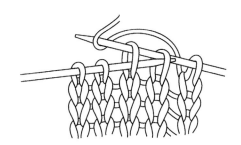

Other

KITCHENER STITCH (GRAFTING)

Bring threaded needle through front stitch as if to purl and leave stitch on needle **(Figure 1)**.

Bring threaded needle through back stitch as if to knit and leave stitch on needle **(Figure 2)**.

Bring threaded needle through first front stitch as if to knit and slip this stitch off needle. Bring threaded needle through next front stitch as if to purl and leave stitch on needle **(Figure 3)**.

Bring threaded needle through first back stitch as if to purl and slip this stitch off needle. Bring needle through next back stitch as if to knit and leave stitch on needle **(Figure 4)**.

Repeat Steps 3 and 4 until no stitches remain on needles.

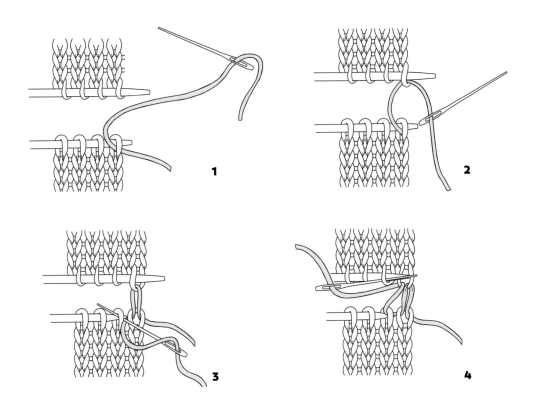

ONE-ROW BUTTONHOLE

With RS facing, bring yarn to front, slip the next stitch purlwise, return yarn to the back, *slip the next stitch purlwise, pass the first slipped stitch over the second slipped stitch and off the needle; repeat from * two more times (Figure 1). Slip the last stitch on the right needle tip to the left needle tip and turn the work so that the wrong side is facing. **With yarn in back, insert right needle tip between the first two stitches on the left needle tip (Figure 2), draw through a loop and place it on the left needle]; rep from ** three more times, then turn the work so the right side is facing. With yarn in back, slip the first stitch and lift the extra cast-on stitch over the slipped stitch (Figure 3) and off the needle to complete the buttonhole.

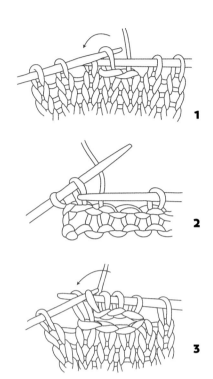

MAGIC LOOP

Cast on stitches as usual, then slide them to the center of the cable, fold the cable and stitches exactly at the midpoint, pull out a loop of cable in the center of the cast-on to make two sets of stitches, then slide each group toward a needle point (Figure 1). Hold the needle tips parallel so that the working yarn comes out of the right-hand edge of the back needle tip. *Pull the back needle tip out to expose about 6" of cable and use that needle to knit the stitches off the front needle (Figure 2). At the end of those stitches, pull the cable so that the two sets of stitches are at the ends of their respective needle tips again, turn the work around, and repeat from *.

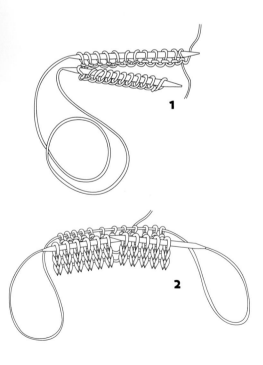

yarn resources

THE BLUE BRICK
shop.thebluebrick.ca

BROOKLYN TWEED
www.brooklyntweed.com

CASCADE YARNS
www.cascadeyarns.com

DONE ROVING
www.doneroving.com

FRABJOUS FIBERS
www.frabjousfibers.com

FREIA FIBERS
www.freiafibers.com

A HUNDRED RAVENS
www. ahundredravens.com

JAMIESON'S OF SHETLAND
www.jamiesonsofshetland.co.uk

JOJOLAND
www.jojoland.com

JUNE PRYCE FIBER ARTS
juneprycefiberarts.blogspot.com

KNITCIRCUS
www.knitcircus.com

MACHETE SHOPPE
www.macheteshoppe.com

SNAILYARN
www.snailyarn.com

SPUN RIGHT ROUND
www.spunrightround.com

SWEETGEORGIA YARNS
www.sweetgeorgiayarns.com

TWISTED FIBER ART
www.twistedfiberart.com

METRIC CONVERSION CHART

TO CONVERT	TO	MULTIPLY BY
Inches	Centimeters	2.54
Centimeters	Inches	.39
Feet	Centimeters	30.5
Centimeters	Feet	0.03
Yards	Meters	0.9
Meters	Yards	1.1

about the contributors

MEGHAN BABIN is the editor of *Interweave Knits*, *knit.wear*, and *Wool Studio*. She enjoys dad jokes, wool, dogs, and craft beer. Follow her on Instagram @meggospurls.

TOBY ROXANE BARNA started her career as a full-time independent knitwear designer in 2012 and, since then, she has released more than 70 patterns and four books. She lives in New York's beautiful Hudson Valley with her cat, Lucy. When not knitting, dyeing yarn, or sewing, she can usually be found (or not) in the woods.

AUD BERGO lives and works in Norway. She has been knitting for more than 40 years but only recently became interested in designing patterns herself. She loves playing with colors and gets inspiration mainly from nature. She prefers knitting warm wearable garments with natural fibers and has a special love for colorwork socks. See all her patterns at www.ravelry.com/designers/aud-bergo/patterns or follow her @softdesign.aud on Instagram.

CAROLYN BLOOM lives in Dobbs Ferry, New York, just a short ride away from Rhinebeck. She is an avid knitter, enthusiastic crocheter, and contented curator of indie-dyed yarn. She has

been knitting for 15 years, always finding time for "just one more row!" See her patterns at www.bloomhandmade studio.com or www.ravelry.com/designers/carolyn-bloom or follow her @bloomhandmadestudio on Instagram.

KAREN BOURQUIN loves living at the ocean's edge on Vancouver Island on the west coast of Canada, where every day is a perfect day to knit, design, and savor the beautiful environment. Find her published designs at www.ravelry.com/designers/karen-bourquin or on her blog at www.docksideknits.wordpress.com.

MARA CATHERINE BRYNER was born and raised in Alaska and now lives with her family in Portland, Oregon. Mara has a background in art and an obsession with color and textiles that eventually turned into an obsession with all things knitting. Her design philosophy involves breaking techniques down to their fundamentals, then building upon those fundamentals in unexpected, unique ways. Her goal is to make knitwear designs that challenge the knitter to create pieces as individual as themselves and help them find their inner textile artist.

ALYSSA CABRERA is a lifelong knitter and has been designing patterns for herself for over a decade. Her grandmother taught her to knit when she was four years old, and she has never stopped. She also dabbles in baking, photography, and destroying the patriarchy. After several major career changes, she finally gave up on the idea of being an employee for someone else and dove headfirst into running her own business. She now owns The Black Purl, a local yarn store in Rochester, New York, where she also lives with her husband and two cats.

TIAN CONNAUGHTON is a designer and technical editor of both knit and crochet patterns, a writer, and teacher. Teaching is at the heart of her approach to design. While her style tends toward classic shapes and silhouettes, her designs are intended to provide learning opportunities featuring interesting and unique details. In addition to her own pattern line, KnitDesigns by Tian (available online), her work frequently appears in knitting and crochet magazines. Tian also created the online courses Pattern Writing 101 and Learn to Grade your Knit and Crochet Pattern using MS Excel. She blogs about crochet, knitting, and design at knitdesignsbytian.blogspot.com.

MEGAN DIAL has been knitting for 15-plus years and crocheting since dinosaurs roamed the Earth (feels like it most days anyway). She enjoys designing new pieces for herself, her wildly imaginative young son, and her fashion-conscious teen daughters, especially "geek" hats and accessories. Megan focuses on working with and highlighting independent spinners, dyers, and other fiber artists who bring new levels of creativity and beauty to the craft.

CAROLINE DICK is a knitwear designer living in British Columbia, Canada. Her designing passions include making the simple look complex and stretching yarn yardage as far as possible.

MONE DRÄGER lives in a village in Germany and loves to craft and be creative. She can't imagine a day without knitting, enjoys playing around with colors and stitch patterns, and has a special fancy for knitted accessories. Find out more about her crafting adventures at www.monemade.com.

In the previous episode of her life, **STELLA EGIDI** was a humanitarian doctor and worked for many years in developing countries. Today, she lives in Rome, Italy, with her husband and two little warriors. Knitwear designing is her way to express herself and her natural inclination to create. She likes experimenting with techniques and creating original, simple, and modern garments and accessories. Her style is quite eclectic, and "moody," as she loves to define herself! You can find her on Ravelry at www.ravelry.com/designers/stella-egidi, Instagram as @moody_knitter, and on her website, www.moodyknitter.it.

KATHRYN FOLKERTH is an independent designer currently living in East Africa. Read about her crafting endeavors at www.KathrynFolkerthDesigns.com.

SUSANNA IC has an extensive collection of studio arts and art history degrees as well as a rather large yarn stash. Her projects and designs can be found on Ravelry and at her website, www.artqualia.com

KYLE KUNNECKE loves stranded knitting. A curious child, he grew up collecting memories of repeating patterns in architecture, and his travels have influenced his designs. Through his online and in-person workshops, he provides inspiration to his students and helps them explore the skills necessary to continue their personal knitting journeys. His first book, *Urban Knit Collection* (Interweave, 2016), explores pattern by using a variety of techniques. He has published designs in magazines and collaborative books, through yarn companies, and under his label, Kyle William. Learn more about Kyle and his work at www.kylewilliam.com.

SARA MATERNINI is the founder and designer of La Cave à Laine (www.lacavealaine.com). Sara is Italian and lives with her family in Alsace, France. She began to knit when she was seven, but later in life she transformed it into a passion and then a job. She is partial to all shades of gray and blue, the right amount of pinks, and all the other colors of the world. She loves to help knitters accomplish their dream shawls in style while having fun. She collects stitch dictionaries, books by Elizabeth Zimmermann, and hand-dyed yarns.

NATALIE SERVANT is an independent knitwear designer with patterns published in print and online. She draws inspiration from architecture, art, and nature. You can see her work at www.natalieservant.ca.

EMMA WELFORD is a knitwear designer in western Massachusetts. When not knitting and playing with color, she is sewing up her dream slow-fashion wardrobe and working on her photography portfolio. Find her online at www.emmawelford.com.

index

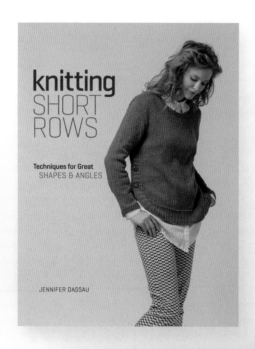
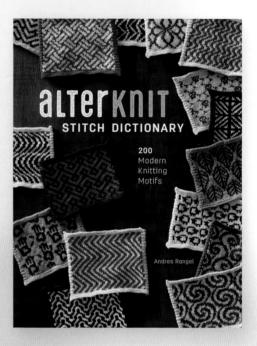
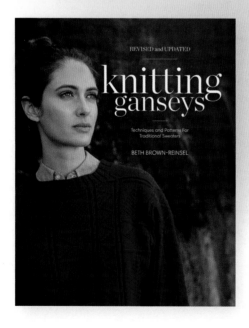